Transvestism and Cross Dressing
Current Views

The Beaumont Trustline
operates on Tuesday and Thursday evenings
between 7 pm and 11pm on
07000 287878

The Beaumont Trust's website can be found at
http://members.aol.com/Bmonttrust/

e_mail *BmontTrust@aol.com*

Transvestism and Cross Dressing

Current Views

Edited by Jed Bland

Beaumont Trust

Transvestism and Cross Dressing
Current Views
Edited by Jed Bland
Published by the Beaumont Trust,
(Registered Charity Number 297527)
BM CHARITY, London WC1N 3XX

Copyright 2004 of the Beaumont Trust
and of the individual authors.

We, the authors who have contributed material to this book, hereby assert and give notice of our rights under Section 88 of the Copyright, Designs and Patents Act 1988, as amended in 2003, to be identified as the authors of the articles published herein under our names.

DISCLAIMER.

In the production of this book, the Beaumont Trust has invited the leading authors in this country to provide material. The Trust has respected their right to their opinions in publishing them unedited, but does not necessarily support them in their entirety.

ISBN 0 9521357 6 0

British Library Cataloguing-in-Publication Data.

A catalogue record for this book is available from the British Library.

Typeset in Monotype Bembo, which is based on a fifteenth century type cut by Francesco Griffo for the Venetian printer Aldus Manutius. Display face Linotype Optima designed by Hermann Zapf and introduced in 1958.

Contents

Foreword *Janett Scott S622* 7
Introduction *Anne Hanson* 9
Preface to the New Edition 12

Labels and Definitions
Transvestism – The Last Taboo *Jed Bland* 15
Why Does Transsexuality Exist? *Alice Purnell* 17
So What is a Transvestite? *Jed Bland* 23
TV, TG, TS – What's in a Label? *Alice Purnell* 27
Are you a cross-dresser or a transvestite? *Jenny Baker* 33

In The Closet
In The Closet *Jed Bland* 39
The Internet Influence on Transfamilies 44
Diana Aitchison BSc.

The Medical Bit
Sexuality and the Transvestite *Jed Bland* 53
The Academic View of Transvestism *Jed Bland* 64
Getting Referred *Dr. Russell Reid* 70

Culture, History and Law
Gender and Cross Dressing across
Time and Culture *Jed Bland* 75
Transvestism, the Church and the Law:
An Historical Review *Vicky (727)* 79
Transvestism and the Church *Revd. David Horton* 106
Transgender and the Law *Stephen Whittle* 116

Counselling and Support
Personally Speaking *Diana Aitchison* — 129
A Cure for Transvestism *Jed Bland* — 136
Relatively Speaking *Diana Aitchison* — 149

Coming Out
Help and Support for Transvestites *Jay Walmsley* — 163
Coming Out *Jed Bland* — 166
The First Time *Jenny Baker* — 167
Passing *Jay Walmsley* — 169
The Joy of Transvestism *Danielle (S4458)* — 173
Into The Open *Jed Bland* — 179
The Police are Only Human
By kind permission of Northern Concord — 181
A Final Word *Jed Bland* — 188
Dangerous Delusions *David Elvy* — 192

Further Reading — 198

Foreword
Janett Scott S622
President for the Beaumont Society

For many years we have had, available, books on Transsexuals or Transsexualism, written as autobiographies by Transsexuals themselves which, although very enlightening, do not cover the many aspects of transvestism and crossdressing. Other books on the subject were inclined to be more from a medical viewpoint and could be misleading.

When this book was first published, it was perhaps one of only three such books that had been published, and the only one left that was still available. In the years that it has been in production it has been an invaluable source of information, for all those who have come into contact with this particular aspect of gender confusion. It has been written by both lay and professional people from the world of the transgendered.

The Beaumont Society, was founded in 1966, as a support group to give help and befriending to other transvestites, crossdressers and transsexuals, as well as their families. The Beaumont Trust came along a couple of years later, made up of Trustees from both the professional and lay fields, to act as a source of information on many gender issues. Over the years there has been a coming together of these ideals within both the Society and the Trust.

Although we have seen over the last twenty years or so, a greater understanding of transvestism and crossdressing, it is still in some ways still seen as some kind of perversion and not fully recognised as a medical condition.

Through the pages of this book, perhaps we can change some of those deep rooted thoughts and fears and bring a greater enlightenment. The leaflets produced by the Society and the Trust can only, because of lack of space, give a brief description, but are in themselves an ideal way to introduce the subject to such other caring organisations such as RELATE, Samaritans and Social Services.

I hope that as you read this book, you will yourself begin to have a greater understanding, but because the subject itself can be very complicated, this book alone can not find all the answers and it can not point to a cure.

Introduction

The Beaumont Trust, a registered charity, was established in 1975 (number 297527), when people working in the field of gender dysphoria came to the conclusion that an independent body, providing help and information was desperately needed.

Excellent work was, and still is, carried out by societies dealing with various aspects of gender dysphoria but no overall umbrella organisation existed to help individuals, many of whom were extremely distressed and fearful, decide which group to turn to and reassure them they were not alone. Indeed many were not even aware of the existence of any groups.

The Albany Trust placed a small office at the Trust's disposal and a telephone helpline was set up, open to callers two evenings a week.

The line was advertised in appropriate journals, through agony aunts, the churches, gay and lesbian switchboards and other caring organisations.

In 1987 the Trust was revised to meet an increasing and more diverse workload. It now handles over 2000 new calls each year.

In addition letters, and now e-mail, are received from those, who for whatever reason, are unable to use a telephone, or who prefer to write. These are all replied to in a caring and informative manner.

The Trust's Press Officer deals with enquiries from the press. Who makes sure they receive fair and accurate information.

The Trust's core activity has always been the dissemination of information and the provision of emotional support to transvestites, transsexuals, transgendered, their wives, partners and families. Giving reassurance and the alleviation of distress.

Where appropriate, and with the caller's consent, the Trust provides referrals to other organisations, professional counsellors and self-help groups. It also helps the individual and his, or her, family and relations to come to terms with the situation and move on.

These conditions are not mental illnesses and are no fault of the individual or their upbringing.

Often highly intelligent, many after years of inner torment, they resolve their lives and go on to be even more useful members of the community.

The Trust's main expenditure is on publicity and the telephone helpline. The helpline provides a national service two evenings a week and is entirely staffed by volunteers. Volunteers and the trustees give their time freely and without payment.

The helpline is a vital service to those in distress and who are sometimes on the point of suicide.

Costs are incurred as calls are transferred. It is however a less expensive way of operating than from a central point, with all the expenses involved in travelling and maintaining an office.

Costs are also incurred in paying psychologists and counsellors to train volunteers and for the publicity needed to make sure, in so far as is possible, the helpline number is known to all who may need it.

This revised book has been produced, to provide information, for individuals and workers in this area by specialists who all have long experience in the field.

It will also, it is hoped, make gender dysphoric persons and those near to them aware they are not alone and they may live full and happier lives.

I must emphasise any communication from an individual to the Trust is completely confidential an any decisions on future courses of action or contacts are only made by the individual concerned.

I am sure all who read this book will benefit form the broad insight they provide into the area of gender dysphoria

I should like to thank the authors on behalf of the trustees for all the hard work they have put into this book on an entirely voluntary and unpaid basis.

The trust also provides free short informative leaflets. To receive them a stamped addressed envelope or other donation to help in the work would be appreciated.

Anne R Hanson
Counsellor
March 2004

Preface to the New Edition

The Beaumont Trusts's Guide to Transvestism was first published some ten years ago. In this edition we have rearranged the chapters, omitting some, in a way which we hope leads logically from what we mean by transvestites, through the problems that many people face, to the experience of 'coming out'. Chapters such as 'Sexuality and the Transvestite' have been split and extended, and new historical, cultural and medical material has been added. Finally, since this edition coincides with the passage of the Gender Recognition Bill through Parliament, the chapter on law has been revised. This legislation, however, mainly affects only those who change role on a permanent basis, and for a more detailed treatment, readers should refer to specialist transsexual literature.

Labels and Definitions

Transvestism: the Last Taboo
Jed Bland

The Beaumont Trust first published its book about transvestism in 1993. It seems incredible that ten years have passed, and even more remarkable is the change in public perceptions that have taken place.

Then, 'transvestite' was a word that was never heard in everyday conversation. Such occasional news reports as there were, would be of a fellow being caught by the Police, walking up the road in a mini-skirt, or pinching underwear off a washing line. Yet there were hundreds, as we say "in the closet". Some simply liked to dress quietly at home, but many others lived in the deepest guilt and emotional distress, frightened to death that someone would find out and, even in everyday life, it would always be in the back of their minds. It was kept hidden from everyone, even fathers, mothers, wives and families. When groups like the Beaumont Society began publicising themselves, they were amazed to find that there were so many others.

We have been accused of painting a gloomy and serious picture, but it was people like these – people who phoned the helpline – that we were writing for. As time has passed, perhaps because of the increasing openness of the subject, particularly on the Internet, the really serious and emotional calls have decreased. Nevertheless, we feel that much of what we have written is as valuable now as it was a decade ago.

Even in the eighties, various figures, such as David Bowie, Boy George and others were challenging the taboos on make up and dress. There is a story that Annie Lennox was stopped at customs in America because she looked like a man. They were, however, perceived as 'showbiz', where anything goes. Then came the Rocky Horror Show. While Tim Curry, as Frank n'Furter, became a cult figure among the 'out' TV population, the closet TV would cringe with embarrassment.

The early 'nineties saw a rash of talk shows, though I doubt they achieved very much, for the people that spoke to us on the helpline simply couldn't relate to them. Two significant media figures, we would submit, were Eddie Izzard, whose comic genius is not dependent on his cross-dressing, and Hayley Cropper, a fictional character in the soap opera *Coronation Street,* who has been accepted as a central character whose transsexualism is no more than an incidental feature of her personality. Finally, an Act to recognise transsexual people in their new gender is currently awaiting the Royal Assent.

There are other books which address the fun of cross dressing, the journals published by the various groups and, of course, the *Tranny Guide*. At the other extreme there has been an endless stream of psychiatric books. While the helpline can discuss everyday problems and provide a confidential space for working through emotional problems, time constraints, if nothing else, limit the opportunity for an extended discussion. We hope that this book will help to fill the gap.

We have also been criticised for paying too much attention to gender identity issues, both by crossdressers and by transpeople. This may be true, to an extent, but for some of the readers of this book there may be a thin line between role-playing and identification.

Why Does Transsexuality Exist?
Alice Purnell

It must be true to say that it is good to like yourself, to be a woman or a man, and feel relaxed and happy about this fact.

Most of the population know and feel that they are happy about their sex and gender, and so they believe people are one or the other; it is in no doubt. Their parents, their body, their sexual identity stated on their birth certificates, clothes and lifestyles all proclaim this clearly to any observer from any country.

"It's a girl" or "It's a boy" is the first and instant definition of who we are. This diagnosis or classification is made at birth, based on the external genitalia alone. It is usually right, plain to see, obvious.

A mother knows it is her baby; she may want a boy or a girl specifically. Above all, though, she wants a healthy, beautiful baby.

It is true that, in many cultures, boys are more valued than girls, but most parents are glad of the gift of a child, who they will love and protect as a part of themselves and confirm their union and continuation. In this millennium in the West, the historical social divides between the two sexes are, at last, less important, and stereotypes are at last being challenged. Girls are allowed to do the things that boys do and may attain the professions and jobs that are traditionally more usually the province of men. The 'new man', Cosmo man if you like, is allowed to cry, to show vulnerability, to be emotional, caring. He is allowed to be an active participant in child care and housework. After all, his wife probably goes out to work too. There are, unfortunately, not enough of these chaps around yet, and the old stereotypes still exist in men and women, government and commercial life.

Why were there different retirement ages, when, on average men die younger than women? Why are 'women's jobs' paid so much less than 'men's'? If all the stereotypes went, but people were regarded as 'different' as men or women, there would still, I feel sure, be millions of people in the world who felt convinced nature had made a mistake, that they were not in accord with their bodies, that they are, in fact, members of the opposite gender and sex. Gender is, I believe, a matter of core identity or personality. Their gender is in no doubt to them. Unfortunately, their body and those around them seem to insist otherwise.

Gender Identity, we gather, is established in a child's mind by the age of two, or at least by four years old. At least she can express it by this age, even the most dull of children. A little boy knows he is a boy before he knows his address, surname, nationality and religion. This is, of course, reinforced by parents, peer groups, dress codes, play and by his name.

Causes of Transsexuality, Gender Dysphoria and Transgenderism, have been postulated by various hypotheses and hypothetical etiologies, some, or all, of which may be significant.

There are two main schools of thought. The nature versus nurture controversy, which runs throughout the study of psychology, ensures that causation is still much in debate. Are gender dysphoric people born or made? I would feel that they are born, and may emerge, given their individual circumstances.

How many just make the best of things and carry on 'as they are supposed to do', without the difficulty overwhelming them? Perhaps it is a matter of degree, some are more dysphoric than others.

The Freudians naturally would assume that the cause of gender dysphoria was based in nurture (upbringing, environmental factors, conditioning etc.) If this is the case, why is there so little evidence for this? They sought to find similar rationales for homosexuality, lesbianism and transvestism, with equal lack of convincing evidence.

By now, in this millennium, homosexuality is not regarded as a deviation, but as a variation, at least by those who are informed, rather than bigoted, but it still has a great stigma attached. In 1990, at the Gay Pride march in London, 50,000 gays and lesbians were able to walk together with pride, despite it being the era of AIDS. One would doubt that transsexuals would get other than ridicule, including from many other 'outsiders'. The public sees it as a curiosity, rather than as a personal tragedy to be overcome. Lack of public sympathy, tolerance and legal equality, with media exposure, all combine to make the lot of transsexuals more intolerable and less understood.

Transsexuals are treated as even more of a bad joke than are gays, or anyone else who is 'different'. This has hampered research into the subject. You cannot have 'flag days' for trannies. Medicine does not see it as a matter of life and death, although the suicide rate is inordinately high.

It seems odd that, so long after the United Nations Charter of Human Rights, that so very many minorities are oppressed, misunderstood, unrepresented, denied civil liberties and rights and are discriminated against by the very laws which are in place, at least in theory, to protect them. Yet our nation, as part of the EEC, and a signatory to the Charter of Human Rights, has denied civil liberties to transsexuals. It has refused to provide documents which might greatly alleviate anxieties and discrimination to our community. While there have been significant changes to the law, one cannot legislate about people's beliefs. Transvestites are treated with great suspicion, generally, though cases are on record, where 'trannies' have been granted custody of children, even though their partner's counsel has set out to use their gender dysphoria as a weapon against them.

The idea of Core Personality is not a new one. In Judeo-Christian terms, one might say 'soul', but it is not quite as simple as that, or as complex. We all know we are an entity, an individual, a member of a particular species, of a particular gender, with a particular sexual orientation and preference. These seem to be critical and more or less fixed elements in an individual personality. One might ask, "What, then, of the hermaphrodite? What of the bisexual? What of the transvestite who makes expeditions into the female mode?" These variations are also elements of the less than rigid reality of nature. You even, rarely, find those whose sex is 'both', it is unclear. You also find those whose sexual preference is towards their own sex, those whose preference swings, even those who feel no attraction for others. Similarly there are those (mainly men) who like, for a time, to pretend that they belong to the opposite sex, but do not necessarily wish to be 'changed over' and do not feel they are in the wrong body.

So how does this tie in with why transsexuality exists? It demonstrates that a variability in sex, gender and sexual orientation exists. The idea of an 'opposite sex' causes much of the confusion, for sex, gender and sexual orientation are more properly spectra, rather than 'black and white'. They are variables throughout nature, not least in humans. It is we humans who apply rigid rules of what is normal, and apply them to the idea of what is good, or somehow morally right. What is, in fact, normal is variability.

So how do gender dysphoric people 'get that way?' The answer, surely, is that they are born as such. What is more important is to address the problem and find ways of coping and of being which are practical and acceptable, and to respect people for being themselves, so long as they do not harm others.

Modern developmental theory suggests that, in the sixth week of gestation (the beginning of the baby's development in her mother's womb) the fetus (unborn baby) will begin to differentiate sexually from the 'female' phenotype. It is interesting that the undeveloped 'neutral' baby seems 'female' to medics. It is, in fact, potentially male or female or (rarely) both. The development towards being a boy is initiated by the Y chromosomes in his cells and by a complex hormonal response. Without this response, a child will appear female, as in testicular feminisation, or have undefined genitals. There is increasing evidence that, at around the same time as sexual differentiation takes place, the brain of the fetus begins to differentiate, possibly in response to this endocrinal stimulation, or lack of it. Brain activity in females and males seems to be differently lateralised, which is said to account for the different gifts and qualities that are averagely attributed to women and men. The rule is that there are always exceptions.

In the gender dysphoria case the person has a mind which tells that person that their gender does not accord with the evidence of their genitals or the chromosomes. A prime part of core personality is core gender conviction. In a developing baby, this is said to begin before birth in response to endocrinal stimuli, and continues with reinforcement from the parents, the mother in particular. In the usual case, a baby boy grows to feel and know he is a boy, and is happy with it. This is, of course, desirable, and the conviction of gender is in accord with and in harmony with what is expected. Not so for the gender dysphoric person. The androgenising effect on the brain is not complete or is absent. Conversely, it would seem in the female to male transsexual, the androgenising effect takes place despite there being no Y chromosome in the baby. This is because the stimulus for this effect comes from the maternal endocrine system.

For a gender dysphoric person, this 'dis - ease' causes great suffering, particularly at puberty. It is nobody's fault. A mother will almost always say or feel "Where did I go wrong?" In fact, nobody went wrong, but a body went 'wrong'. It is just that the core gender conviction of such a person has placed them in the horrifying and wonderful situation of breaching that fundamentally wrong divide of people into two sexes. We are, after all, everyone in this world, made up so many complex elements, some 'male', some 'female', some both and some neither.

So What is a Transvestite?
Jed Bland

From time to time the helpline will be asked "I have discovered that I like to wear my wife's tights and knickers from time to time. Am I turning into a transvestite?" As Professor Joad might have said "It depends what you mean by transvestite."

The word was first coined by Magnus Hirschfeld in 1910. He was a controversial figure, particularly because of his openness about his own homosexuality, and his campaigning for homosexual tolerance. Three months after Hitler became Chancellor, in 1933, the "Nazi Committee against the Un-German Spirit" broke into his Institute in Berlin and destroyed it. Modern documentaries often feature film from the time of the burning of the Institute's library, including no doubt copies of his book *Transvestites*. The book describes a number of people who spent long periods living and working as the opposite sex. One wonders whether any of them would have asked for medication and surgery if it had been available.

Transvestism has a long history, even in England. Garber, in *Vested Interests,* describes how cross dressing was common in Elizabethan England, yet was proscribed under King James I. Students of Shakespeare know of his fascination with the idea of experimenting with gender crossing. It would not have been such a feature of his work if it had not struck a chord with his audience. Many of his plays feature male actors playing the part of a woman playing the part of a man. The recent film *Shakespeare in Love* turns the idea on its head with a woman playing the part of a man playing a woman.

By Victorian times, it had been driven underground, along with all forms of sexual expression. Money records how breakfast cereals were invented to encourage 'clean living', while masturbation was claimed to induce 'feeble-mindedness.' With this background of guilt, people would look for professional help. They became case histories and transvestism became pathologised.

In the twentieth century the Diagnostic and Statistical Manual (DSM) of the American Psychiatric Association, defined only the fetishistic transvestite among the erotic deviations, and the transsexual, a distinction that many transsexuals have seized on to justify their position. Brierley first described what he called the *Dual Role Transvestite* as a social, rather than a erotic phenomenon. Later Bancroft, in his enormous textbook *Human Sexuality and its Problems,* classified transvestism into four categories: Fetishistic Transvestites, Gay transvestites, Dual Role Transvestites and Transsexuals.

Another cultural myth which needs to be disposed of right away is the perceived link between transvestism, of whatever kind, and homosexuality. One may be homosexual without being a transvestite and the reverse is also true. Another piece of terminology is Heterosexual Transvestite, to emphasise the fact that they are quite clear about their sexual attraction exclusively to the opposite sex.

In passing, one might consider a transsexual woman who is attracted to men. Does she change from being homosexual to being heterosexual? Those who remain attracted to women have been forced to refer to themselves as 'lesbian transsexuals', which has not endeared them to feminist writers. The literature has been made even more confusing, by the practice of reassigning boy infants and bringing them up as girls, for various reasons, blurring the distinction between male and female and hence between heterosexuality and homosexuality. For completeness then, we will mention two other terms, *androphilic* and *gynephilic,* which you may find in some academic papers. Also, whereas transsexual people have traditionally been referred to as "male to female" or "female to male", some prefer the terms *transwoman* and *transman*.

In recent years, there has been a decided move towards using the euphemism 'cross-dresser', the inference being that it is simply dressing-up and no more – a bit of 'manly' fun. This is in contrast to Brierley's Dual Role Transvestite, who, while dressed as a woman 'is' a woman in his mind. In truth there are a multitude of motives (and benefits) of breaking the mould, as recorded in Marriette Pathy Allen's beautiful, though expensive, book *Transformations*.

Consider too, Marcie.M., in the American journal Tapestry;

"I began to realize that I did not have to rely on a façade of macho bluster and masculine charm to get along in the world. In my professional life I began to develop my own management style. This in itself was a unique idea in the hidebound paramilitary industry where I worked. I tried to be fair and even-handed with my crews, and was pleasantly surprised when the results were very good. My men repaid me with a loyalty I'd never experienced, and excellent job performances. I guess part of this process was really just maturing. My personal life was delivering me plenty of hard knocks, and they were also chipping away my rough edges. My crossdressing began also to change. I sought out the help of many people in my original goal of becoming more passable. I had started out thinking I was looking for technical advice. What I was lucky to find were people willing to like me and offer me the encouragement and support I needed to find value in myself. I found through these caring people the strength to be confident in myself, and to walk in the world with pride. I discovered the inner strength that I had been denying. I learned to accept myself, and was gratified to discover that other people, especially those I love, could accept me too.

I started out trying to find shoes that fit and the right way to apply blusher - I wound up discovering my soul."

This is clearly is more than just dressing up, nor is it sexual fetishism, but it isn't transsexualism.

Another word that has been increasingly used in recent years is *transgender*. Originally a transgenderist was someone who lived full time in the opposite role without surgery or medication. Nowadays it describes a community of people who cross between gender roles in one way or another. Many have adopted the word 'tranny'. It is a more comfortable word which does not force one to label oneself too rigidly. Even some transsexual people have been heard to use it about themselves.

In the end perhaps, it is only a problem because we see it as a problem. Recently, in the news, there was an account of an man, an ex-war hero, who had quietly decided to live the rest of his life as a woman, without approaching any doctors, and had done so. It will recalled that the Chevalier d'Eon Beaumont lived his life also as a woman (and is regarded as transvestite not transsexual) In both cases their physiological sex was only discovered after their death.

Books mentioned in this chapter.
Magnus Hirschfeld, (1910) *Transvestites: The erotic drive to cross-dress*. English translation by Michael A. Lombardi-Nash, (1991) Prometheus Books

Allen, Marriette Pathy, (1990) *Transformations: Crossdressers and Those Who Love Them,* Dutton Books.

Marcie M., (1995) *In search of my soul.* from *Tapestry,* Issue 70, Winter 95, Massachusetts: International Foundation for Gender Education

TV, TG, TS
What's in a Label?
Alice Purnell

While it is true that the transvestite or the fetishist for that matter, may start off wearing female clothes and experimenting even in childhood, it does not follow that if a little boy puts on one of Mummy's frocks he will turn out to be a transvestite, a fetishist, an homosexual, a transgenderist or a transsexual.

This type of behaviour is not uncommon in small children, who experiment in so many ways. A TV or a TS is most probably going to be secretive about dressing up; it is too important in the child's mind not to be uneasy about it.

So if a man puts on a dress is he an homosexual? Is he a transsexual? Is he crazy? Is he doing something wrong? If he likes certain items of traditionally female clothes to wear is he a transvestite?

At least with the labels we can answer some of these questions.

There are many more men that have fetishes than there are transvestites. Is it a progression? The answer is no and yes, if we view fetishism as a part of sexual play. Certainly the first exploration into fetishism may light the transvestite fire as it were.

Few fetishists would be prepared to try to look like a woman, or to go out in public dressed up, unless they had a strong exhibitionist streak. Most are content to use their fetish for sexual stimulation in masturbation or with a consenting partner.

So what of the man who wants to dress and behave as he thinks a woman does? He is probably a transvestite.

What of the very effeminate sissy-boy type of child? Recent research indicates that he is more likely to grow up as an effeminate homosexual, the drag queen type, but he might not.

Most transvestites are otherwise fairly ordinary men, who have this, often secret almost other self. 'She' is often a fantasy woman, one he so seeks that he identifies with her to the extent that he becomes 'her' from time to time. It could be said that transvestism is the ultimate in heterosexuality, where he becomes the one he might fancy, the fantasy woman. It would seem that the majority of transvestites are heterosexual, most marry, most lead fairly conventional lives apart from their TV thing.

It is true that, when dressed up, some do exhibit an intermittent homosexuality. Some who would not dream of having an affair with another man do experiment when dressed up, with other TV's or sometimes with non-TV men, but again this seems to be the minority rather than the majority.

This idea of a dual personality, even speaking of his 'female' self as though she were another person is a device often used by both the TV and his partner. It reinforces this almost magical notion of being someone else, whilst not being a multiple personality disorder, it is at the same time confusing.

What if he wants to live all the time as a woman? This sort of person could be regarded as a chronic (in the medical sense) transvestite, or may be a transgenderist. The transgenderist is a full-time transvestite sometimes or may be a person for whom the transsexual options can not be a reality for practical reasons like health, age, size, inability to 'pass'.

So it seems that transgenderism may not be a syndrome but a solution.

What of the full-time Transvestite? 'She' is happy to present as a woman but has no deep inclination to have reassignment surgery. 'She' may either be a phallic woman as seen in TV/TS erotica, or a gender motivated transvestite who is just happier that way, or she may merely have been forced to this compromise by her circumstances.

So what if he takes female hormones – is he becoming a woman? Not necessarily. He may be being diagnosed, employing the idea that the TV often stops a dressing urge when given estrogens by a Gender Identity Clinic, for example. It can clarify matters for a psychiatrist, since there seems to be a libidinal link to the need to dress in the case of the TV, rather than in the TS, whose need to change her body to confirm with her core personality as a woman does not diminish.

TV's may go to great lengths to 'pass', even having hormones, shaving, waxing, sugaring away body hair, spending a great deal of time and money to achieve what he perceives as his female inner self. Is he a narcissist, in love with himself? Sometimes this is the case but, like all chaps with a 'hobby', he wants to get it right.

Sadly, having been spared the criticism of other teenage girls as any ordinary girl might, the TV is often rather stereotypical, may sometimes wear a dress that suits him, often old fashioned, but sometimes like mutton dressed up as lamb. The point is, that he dresses for himself, not to seek a man, nor sensibly to do the multitude of things a modern woman does.

The TV is not a woman, he just likes to dress as one. I say 'he' because there are very few female transvestites. These days, women can wear what they want, when and where they want. Some look great in DJ. Not too many men look good in a strapless evening dress. This says something about our conditioning in terms of what is fashionably acceptable.

Women have more dress freedom. Men have more financial freedom. Women are taken as images rather than as people in their own right, they have to be attractive, men can look like slobs yet will be treated far more seriously than a woman who dresses like a tart or a dyke. The sex war is very clearly established in all our childhoods. TV's TS's and ordinary men and women are all victims of this nonsensical stereotyping and confusion.

Does a Transvestite eventually want to be a transsexual? There is a not unnatural fear among the families that transvestites become TS, but this fear is as unfounded as the fear that he might 'become' an homosexual. In a sense homosexuals are born and not made. The same could be said of the transsexual (and the TV for that matter). Indeed Transsexuals often will dress as the 'Opposite Sex', but they would maintain with some accuracy that they were dressing as themselves. They do not put on women's clothes, they put on their own clothes, for their gender is in accord with these clothes, which are worn to express their complete personality, not just a part of it.

Sadly many TV's are so guilt ridden about 'dressing' that they convince themselves and try to convince psychiatrists that they are in fact TS. After surgery if they are unfortunate enough to achieve their misplaced goal it is too late to go back surgically, though some do try to make a go of it as men socially and at work. Tragically others kill themselves with drink or by more dramatic forms of suicide.

So many men have almost no concept of what it is actually like to be a woman twenty four hours a day. You have only to hear TV's, then their wives, talking, to hear the very apparent vast divide between topics of conversation TV's have and a wife's awareness of being a woman and thinking like one.

A man who has failed as a person may think life is easier as a woman. It is not. It is different. A post-operative TS is in a disadvantageous position as a woman, yet has all the ordinary pressures of being a woman in an unequal society, together with all the prejudices directed at her by the state, the media, the legal system and society in general to cope with. She may also not 'pass' and be isolated from others by this. It is also probable that getting employment will be difficult, finding a loving and understanding partner hard. Acceptance by a partner, parents and children will not always be easy. 'Women's Work' is poorly paid and under-rated, often being based on image rather than ability.

Often a great deal is lost for the TS to find herself, or himself for that matter. The price in emotional terms can also be very high. She has to be certain.

Can the TS be regarded as a chronic TV? Not really. The two conditions are different. They have similarities, but so do a headache and meningitis.

If you asked a TV "Which would you have rather been born as, a boy or a girl?", most would probably say "As a woman", without knowing what a woman was, but knowing that he could wear what he liked to wear, women's clothes. The TS's answer might be the same, but she is more likely to say, or mean, "As a normal woman", without any necessary reference to clothes. She feels nature has made a profound mistake, but she is certain she is a woman. Sex and gender are actually very different polarities, they may be in accord or not. Degrees of masculinity and femininity exist in all of us. Humans are complex creatures and there is no absolute.

Ask a TV if he would like to have periods and he would probably say "No". Ask some women and you would get the same answer. Ask a TS and she would almost always say "Yes". Ask a female to male TS if he minds that he will probably be afflicted by male-pattern baldness, because of his testosterone injections, he will be delighted. It helps him to look authentic. Few other men would be so pleased. To be a TV or a TS often means a great deal of self-deception. We might do well to accept that it is part of the variability of life. Some people just might be 100% normal, (or, better, a hundred per cent average) but I have never met one. Perhaps that is why people are so fascinating.

So why are labels important? TV's and TS's are like any labelled group, they come in all shapes and sizes, with the full spectrum of types and choice of sexual partner and sexuality, with varying ability at 'passing'. All deserve respect, sometimes sympathy, often understanding, as do their partners and families.

Are you a cross-dresser or a transvestite?

Jenny Baker
(Group co-ordinator of the Northern Concord)

Call me an old fashioned girl, but I've always been rather taken with eonism as the term that should have been adopted for cross-dressing.

Eonism was first coined in the late 19th century by Havelock Ellis, one of those great 'psychosexual pioneers' who declared that cross-dressers were not just mildly eccentric, as we had been considered for centuries before, but really mentally afflicted.

It was thanks to the likes of him, Freud and Krafft-Ebing that cross-dressers discovered that they were actually suffering from something, when all the time they had thought they were just enjoying it. And now they had a condition, there had to be a name for it.

Eonism, of course, comes from the Trust's 'patron saint', the Chevalier D'Eon, also known as Madame Lia de Beaumont, the celebrated cross-dressing secret agent. The Chevalier was a cool number. If we have to be classed as something, being an eonist doesn't seem too bad a moniker.

For a while, we almost were. Eonism ran head to head in the psycho-babble world for some years with its main rival 'transvestism', but lost out to the far less prosaic term. We weren't to be followers of a daredevil in drag, just mental defectives that 'trans-vestis' - simply cross-dress in Latin.

By terming it transvestite, the psychoanalysts not only managed to create a mental condition that hadn't been recognised before, but in one fell swoop took in every form of cross-dressing around. A brilliant marketing coup if ever there was one.

So it is that the term transvestite has such negative connotations. It is a word created to describe an affliction that upsets people's lives, breaks up marriages and is generally thought to be just the tip of the iceberg for what other degenerate practices go on in unseen places.

Speak the name with a nod and a wink, as people do when they think they know what's associated with it. Unless you ask them directly of course, and suddenly they don't really know. Funny aren't we, us humans?

The little realisation that men who put on frocks do it for 1001 different reasons of their own has just started to dawn on people who actually take the time to think about it.

The problem is that each of these cross-dressers is also a human being, with strangely enough, minds of their own and thought patterns unique to them. The only real thing they have in common is their personal drive to wear women's clothes, which is fundamental to them.

We can't attribute a reason as to why people like the things they do other than the simple motive of reward. People do a certain thing because it does something for them. Something beneficial, something pleasurable, something that removes pain or stress, something that helps them survive, but bottom line because they get enjoyment from it.

Is it the demonstration of his feminine personality; is it escapism from the stresses of being a male in today's society? Is it purely a tactile thing, or just a sexual turn-on? Ask enough cross-dressers and you'll find all of these reasons and lots more besides.

With so many reasons, perhaps it's not surprising that so many different terms are now being put forward. We've had enough of being lumped together as "transvestite" - and I suppose the old Chevalier is a bit passé as a role model - so we're coming up with names of our own.

These include "transpeople", "transpersons" or "transgendered", which in the modern day idiom means perhaps that they feel they are more than just the manifestation of a man in women's clothes. They feel their personality is part way between the gender divide and that puts them one rung up the ladder from a cross-dresser. Perhaps you could call them a cross-dresser with attitude.

Are the pioneers of modern day cross-dressing seeing another nuance in the evolutionary process? Or is it just that you can now apply your own label these days to make you feel better? Perhaps organic 'cross-dresser', unaffected by the fertiliser that life throws at you?

One of the better titles I've heard applied by a prominent full-time cross-dresser is "Gender Gifted", enjoying the best of both worlds. Not gone down the road of the transsexual in wanting to surgically change their appearance to that of a woman, but still lives full time in role.

The term 'transsexual', of course, doesn't really fit with the others. Or does it? Is a cross-dresser's desire to dress up and look as much like a woman as possible just a weaker form of the transsexual's "I believe I am a woman"? Is dressing in women's clothes just the first step to becoming a transsexual, like a progressive illness?

Well, out of all the probabilities and possibilities this one has an answer; there is a difference between a 'true' transsexual and a good cross-dresser. One believes they should have been a woman from birth and the other just gets enjoyment from doing what he does to whatever degree he does it.

Although cross-dressing is progressive from the first pair of knickers to the latest imitation fur stole, it doesn't lead on to transsexualism, although a sad number of confused people may have thought so to their later regret.

So what's in a name? For that answer, let's refer to the Northern Concord's web site where we have a form for people to complete about themselves for publication in *Cross Talk* magazine. One of the questions there is "What Do You Prefer To Be Called?"

A drop-down box gives the possible options of 'cross-dresser', 'transvestite', 'transgendered', 'transsexual' and finally 'none of them – I don't like titles'. By far and away the largest majority of Concord members choose the last option.

There's no doubt that everyone is getting fed up with being pigeonholed. Perhaps it's time to just class the condition that we all share as simply 'human'.

In The Closet

In the Closet
Jed Bland

A two-or three year-old learns that there are two kinds of person and that he, or she, belongs to one of them. Thus the child may be able to tell you that it is a boy or girl, but it doesn't mean very much. A boy believes he could become a girl if he wanted to by playing girls games or wearing dresses or growing hair long, and vice versa. Some time between four and six years, comes the understanding one stays in the same gender throughout life. It seems that, between the ages of three and about six, there is a period of experimentation, as a child sets out to find out what the gender-concept means. Nursery nurses often speak of little boys who select little girls' clothes in dressing-up games.

For most, it is simply experimentation. For a few boys, there is a persistent preference for female stereotyped toys and behaviour. Most such children will become gay, but there are some few children who can never adapt themselves to their assigned role and become transsexuals. Similarly for girls, though it seems that cross-gender stereotyped behaviour is more tolerated in girls than in boys.

A large peer group provides a wide range of models, yet it must be one that can accommodate the child as he, or she, is. Possibly, socialisation is harder for a boy. Though there is no doubt that good deal of hen-pecking goes on among girls, they tend to remain solitary, with perhaps one or two 'best friends'. Boy's society tends to be organised in gangs, and a boy has to be successful in gaining entrée to one, or another, élite.

Many transvestites say they began dressing at around eight, when a child usually realises that he is stuck with the gender he has - gender constancy. Others say they started in puberty.

Both of these ages, in everyone, seems to coincide with some sort of life change, not only social, but in the body chemistry. Clearly at such an early age, it has little do with eroticism, though the ritual of cross dressing may, in teenage, become highly arousing. However, there some who that they first found themselves trying on some clothes in adulthood, often after a crisis, like divorce or bereavement.

What such children know from the beginning is that they shouldn't say anything about it, and go to the most amazing lengths to hide their activities, cross-dressing for years, unknown to their closest family. Some secret TV's are literally paranoic about discovery. While dressing, they imagine that people can see through curtains, through walls. They jump at every creak of the floorboards. Afterwards, they worry about whether they've removed the make up properly, or if they've remembered to put everything away. The release of cross dressing is replaced by the fear of discovery, the guilt and secrecy. They feel that social attitudes are such that they dare not speak of it to anyone.

Feelings that cannot be expressed take on an undeniable urgency. They may be safely tucked away in denial and suppression for years, then surface in times of stress. When the transvestite does express them, the pressures that told him he mustn't have those feelings as a man also tells him he mustn't act them out as a woman - a classical Catch 22 situation. Often there is denial. He tries to forget it and pretend it isn't true, but little everyday happenings trip his memory and he gets an unreasoning fear that, somehow, people 'know' about him, like having the mark of Cain. Even dressing brings only temporary relief. In the first edition I wrote that a system may be set up, where feelings of 'not being a man' conflict with the urge to dress, followed by a session of relief dressing, followed by a reaction in becoming over macho, followed in turn by guilt, in a downward spiral of emotional distress.

The need becomes an obsession, distracting from everyday life. Efforts to control, like 'wardrobe burning', fail repeatedly. The transvestite will tell lies and will become less 'present' for his family. Even in the face of direct confrontation he will deny the problem, even the physical fact of the cross-dressing.

This, of course, has all the hallmarks of addiction, and it is often labelled as such. One obvious difference is that chemical addiction usually produces physiological changes, often such as to perpetuate the addiction. It is arguable that, in this 'closet' situation, cross-dressing produces similar psychological changes, leading to a loss of value for the male life and a glamorisation of the female life. But the vital difference is that addiction is often an escape from feelings, while cross-dressing may, in part, be an enactment of them.

The person may attempt other escapes, through alcohol, drugs, tranquillisers, workaholism. He will, in addition, be prey to those conditions, neurotic and medical, which are considered to be exacerbated by stress.

With the opportunity to express his feelings more freely, the compulsion to do so is reduced, along with the obsession, and becomes seen as simply a need. Those transvestites that have already 'come out' have unthinkingly followed this process, giving themselves, not only permission to dress, but permission to be 'different' and permission to explore feelings.

It may be that, in the last few years, with the increasing visibility of cross-gender people, transvestites do not get to this point before asking for help. If so, the previous editions will have gone some way towards achieving their purpose.

The Internet has had an important influence, as it has in so many areas of life. It is a virtually limitless source of information and has allowed people, who would otherwise be isolated, to communicate with each other.

In December 1993, a transman named Brandon Teena was murdered in America. Ordinarily such an event would have passed largely un-noticed as it had so many times before. In fact, the local police had been instructed to take no action. A local net user heard about it and circulated the news, which resulted in several vigils of support by transgender activists, attracting television coverage and the attention of news media around the world.

Many transsexual people have merged into the general community and can share thoughts that they could not discuss publicly. They tend to be scattered widely around the country, as they are around the world. The facility to communicate through forums and newsgroups has allowed them to co-ordinate their efforts into comprehensive campaigns, as with the British group, Press for Change.

At the same time, it is clear that there are some pretty opinionated people out there. Most of the e-mail groups have experienced "flame wars" from time to time, which could be very upsetting if one took them seriously. This is particularly true of chatrooms which one should approach with a deal of caution. The world is not a pretty place, and there some vindictive folk who will play on people's weaknesses, if they can discover them. There are stories of people who have been driven to the point of nervous breakdown.

On the Internet itself, there are websites of every imaginable kind. Most users are able to put up their own homepage, and link it to collections of others. There are also informational sites from elementary school educational pages to archives of academic papers. As with newspapers and television documentaries, one can write almost anything without having to actually justify it in established theory. One needs to be particularly wary of those that claim to be scientific, but are actually selling something, or have some hidden political agenda.

It is also easy to forget that, nowadays, one can doctor photographs in all sorts of ways. Even in the past, before electronic editing reached its present sophistication, Sam Fox, the Page Three pinup, pointed out that the models had their breasts formed into shape with sticky tape, which was airbrushed out before the picture was published. What is interesting is that, in spite of the advances in Internet graphics, the text archives like 'Fictionmania' have never lost their appeal.

There are websites catering for every imaginable fantasy scenario. They take away much of the guilt and isolation, and could be said to be no different from in substance from adult magazines, except that the latter have a limited number of pages, and one has to go out and buy them. Similarly, though there are clubs and commercial establishments in the real world, one has to look for them and work up the courage to visit them, when on the net they are available at the click of a mouse.

In this virtual closet, people may become 'sissy maids' or participate in forced feminisation scenarios. They may invent Internet fantasy personae and, for most it is simply an escape – and to some extent it is no different from other hobbies that 'take over' – but, for some, their fantasy persona becomes their 'real' identity.

One area that is driving the Internet is mail-order shopping. There are sites specifically for cross dressers, while many female fetish sites have sections catering for transvestites, all usually extremely expensive. However, many of the mainline mail order houses now have an Internet presence.

The Internet Influence on Transfamilies
Diana Aitchison BSc.

I once started an essay by stating that 'the Internet is a wonderful thing for researchers' and indeed it is. I can find information on virtually any subject available globally (including a few I'd rather not know about!). There is no doubt that it is the most life enriching tool that has been made available to almost everyone since the first dictionary was published. However, like all good things there is a down side to the Internet that has dominated the calls to Women of the Beaumont Society in the last two years. The following is a sample concern;

"I've known about my husband's crossdressing for years and after the initial shock had worn off, I started to join in and accompany him to various social events. I thought that he was the average tranny and many people said that he was very well balanced so I didn't think that we had any problems.

Now though, he has discovered the Internet and since we installed it a few months ago my husband has changed dramatically. He stays up all night surfing and is consequently becoming worn out which is making him irritable. He has also become very secretive. We first started together looking for other couples like ourselves who we could share our cross dressed experiences with but he soon got fed up with that and now won't let me in on the sites that he finds. In fact he has set up a separate screen name and password which locks me out. Apart from the secretiveness I'm also concerned that he will lose his job as he has recently had a written warning about being late and performing badly. He has been with the firm for 15 years and they are at a loss to understand why he has gone downhill so quickly.

There are other issues too. He no longer wants to make love and has changed from a loving out going person into an introverted stranger who doesn't want to go anywhere except to meetings and clubs and now he doesn't ask me to go with him anymore. Things have come to a head because he won't come on holiday with me and the children unless he can buy a very expensive lap-top that he can access the Internet and e-mails on and costs more than the actual holiday. I've begged him to give the computer a break and get some proper sleep again while we are away but he just snarls at me and says that I am being selfish. He says that he cannot see any harm in having a hobby. I feel so excluded that I can't see any point in us staying married."

This wife has described an obsessional interest in something that distracts her husband from normal married life. It is probable that the same thing is happening in families where cross-dressing is not present. Parents frequently complain about the time that children spend on surfing the Internet which they feel prevents a natural interaction and socialisation process outside the home. However, in the case of the wives who call there is an additional factor – the dramatic change in their husband's personalities. There are physical concerns too; obsessed surfers soon complain of eyestrain, headaches and the features usually present in sleep deprivation such as short attention spans, lack of concentration, poor short term memories and mood swings.

A study by Dr. Donald Black of the University of Iowa (published in the American *Journal of Clinical Psychiatry*) and reported by James Chapman (Daily Mail, 9/2/2000) suggests that compulsive computer usage 'can increase the chances of psychiatric illness by more than four times.' In the same edition of the Daily Mail, a leading female divorce lawyer, Vanessa Lloyd Platt, states 'Divorce: Why we women are to blame', going on to argue that it is women's new found aggression (assertiveness) that is to blame for marital breakdowns and women should learn to be more submissive.

The most dramatic effects of compulsive behaviours on family life are the 'drip drip' effect that wears down a wife psychologically. Initially she may just be irritated by his obsession with the Internet but as her concerns are rebuffed she can experience deep emotional hurt and feelings of rejection. Children may start to notice the change in both parents and the wife will struggle to maintain the status quo, often to the extent of lying on behalf of her husband. Questions such as "Mummy, why doesn't Dad sleep in your bed any more?" or "I'm sure I can hear the click of the mouse when I'm asleep - why does Daddy stay on the computer all night?" and probably the worst complaint from a mother's point of view: "Why is Daddy too tired to take us anywhere any more?" can be distressing and guilt forming to a wife who believes that truthfulness is everything in parenting. The greatest fear for some wives is that because their husbands are usually cross-dressed for their nocturnal activities there is a real danger that one of the children may wake up and investigate their father's whereabouts, thus catching him en femme.

Ultimately the strain will take its toll with wives worn down by lack of emotional support from their spouses to the point where they are virtually ignored. One wife related that she knew that her marriage was in trouble when her husband only communicated with her through e-mails and that it was in such a way that she realised that she had been reduced to the role of housekeeper and nanny.

Having come to recognise the possible permanence of the night time regime, wives will turn their attention to the content of the sites that their husbands are so interested in. Where wives have managed to gain entry to their husband's domain they have been appalled to discover the pornographic nature of the material that they have down loaded. E-mails often provide an insight too into the fantasy world that has taken over their husband's rationale. In worst case scenarios husbands have adopted a totally new identity who lives only in Cyberspace where they are gorgeous 'she-males' or single 'girls' with exciting life styles who love to flirt and engage in romantic liaisons, at least electronically. Many will be displaying a keen interest in hormones and plastic surgery; a significant number may have started a covert self-medication regime by accessing the required products through the Internet.

Not all the wives will be conscious of their husband's need to crossdress, so discoveries such as these can be severely debilitating. Such is the shock of discovery of the depths of their husbands' duplicity that wives can be reduced to a shadow of their former selves in a very short time. Symptoms such as changes in their menstrual cycle/frequency, an inability to articulate properly, short-term memory loss and shortness of temper where a wife was previously viewed to be even-tempered and easy going are commonly mentioned. Some may be presented for mental illness brought on by the stressful events following the emotional disclosure of their husband's secret.

The over all effect on family life can be dramatic particularly when the husband ceases all pretence at preserving the traditions associated with family life. Sadly, when cornered he is likely to blame his wife for 'everything'; such is his confused state that he can no longer differentiate fact from fantasy and consequently resents his wife's interruption of his well-ordered world. The images from the material viewed, the nature of the contacts made in chat rooms and the self-seeking commentaries on lists have served to reinforce his gender dysphoria to the extent that they become the sole focal point of his day-to-day existence. The obsessive/compulsive nature of the behaviour in some men has led them towards the realms of dissociative disorders where they can deny their real life existence as husband and father to the extent of wishing only to be called by their female name in their domestic domain. Consequently wives find that they have to become assertive in their wishes for a normal family life that excludes the children from access to their father's alter ego. The family budget is undermined by the expensive purchasing of wigs and breast prostheses via Internet shopping sites designed specifically for cross-dressers, causing further scope for assertiveness from wives who are at their wits end trying to balance the books.

Ultimately, marriages will fail under the pressure of the duality of the husband's persona. Outwardly he remains family man, husband and father, reliable employee and pillar of society. Behind closed doors he is a self-obsessed stranger who shirks his domestic role in order to embrace the world he believes he truly belongs to. He may believe that his wife will indulge his passions for cyber life as long as he maintains the family home at least financially. He may even convince himself that he is entitled to his private world after a stressful day earning the family's daily bread. He will undoubtedly suffer periods of guilt when he rationalises his behaviour but may convince himself that he 'can't help it – after all there are thousands on the Net just like him so it must be normal behaviour'. He may also recognise the adrenaline runs that can be achieved through accessing his secret world; an addictive factor in its self. Negative forces such as denial and guilt may subsequently lead to levels of clinical depression and an inability to function normally any more, thus culminating in loss of employment and further strain on the family. A gender dysphoric man who is undertaking the practises defined here should clearly be thinking about seeking the appropriate help in the form of counselling from professionals in the field that would include his wife so that she may too be helped.

Perhaps if Dr. Black and Vanessa Lloyd Platt were to join forces we might one day find an answer on how to combat the forces that encourage women to be assertive (sic aggressive) in the face of Internet influences on their loved ones that seek through the promotion of addictive, compulsive practices to destroy marriages and family life.

Previously published in the Gendys Journal, Issue 10, May 2000.
http://www.gender.org.uk/gendys/2000/10diana.htm

The Medical Bit

Sexuality and the Transvestite
Jed Bland

Some transvestite groups become very defensive as soon as anyone uses the word 'sex', while others acknowledge, and embrace, the eroticism inherent in challenging gender mores.

Throughout the literature the terminology is unacceptably sloppy. Thus the words 'sex' and 'gender' are used interchangeably, with the latter as a euphemism for the former. There is a website that claims to tell you how to tell the 'gender' of your hamster. It does, of course, prevent search engines from restricting it to the adult pages.

Fundamental to the confusion about the word 'sex' is that most people take it to refer to the sex act itself. When science (including Freud) writes about sex they mean the differences in physiology and behaviour between males and females, correctly called 'sexual dimorphism'. Gender is not just whether one is male or female, but the way male and female people describe and portray themselves and each other in terms of being masculine or feminine. Thus recently it has become usual to refer to 'sexual identity' as the knowledge one is male or female, while 'gender identity' is the feelings about oneself as masculine or feminine. Thus we have no problem with the word 'transsexual' as someone who changes their sex *role*.

Sexual Fantasy

Although we have come a long way since Victorian times in terms of sexual negativism, we still have a long way to go. Reiss, with typical American simplicity, boils it down to one simple phrase, "equality in relationships with responsibility to avoid harm."

Once the boy reaches physical sexual maturity, cross-dressing is likely to be extremely erotic. Fantasies involving cross-dressing may be alternated, from time to time, with ordinary heterosexual fantasies focusing on particular women. Possibly, for those who have started cross-dressing at an earlier age, the experience is more familiar. Psychological arousal is not so great, and, for them, the erotic component is not so important. While some spend many years questioning themselves, other just do it.

The emphasis, of course, is that fantasies will be explored within a relationship, but there are many people who, for perfectly good reasons, cannot find one. They may be disabled in one way or another, or they may be shy or physically unattractive. They may simply be out of work and feel that they have nothing to offer a prospective partner. But why should they be deprived of the right to sexual fantasy?

This is Freud's description of children's play: Play is motivated behaviour, caused by the child's feelings both conscious and unconscious.

The child, under normal circumstances, can distinguish play from reality, but uses objects and situations from the real world to create a world of its own that is comfortable. Pleasant experiences can be repeated at will. Events may be altered in the way in which it finds most pleasing.

Sexual fantasy is adult play. Few people are immune to the urges of their endocrine system. In experiencing the sexual feelings, other feelings, long suppressed, may come through. Thus they construct their sexual daydream, from past events and experiences. What we are doing is to give permission to work through these feelings and experiences and find a resolution.

Fetishism

From early significant experiences, fetishes, or paraphilias, may begin. Someone may become attached to the smell and feel of rubber, another to being tied up, another to women's underwear, sometimes the old-fashioned directoire knickers with elastic around the legs. Many transvestites have a passion for items of clothing. Many will proudly display collections of two hundred pairs of shoes (Britain's answer to Imelda Marcos?) or possess fifty or more pairs of panties.

Some transvestites go on to rituals that they may have read about, female dominance (or male), sissy boy, schoolgirl or French Maid scenarios. Usually these are more to do with experimenting with power in relationships, rather than gender issues. In such 'open' fetishism, the sexual rituals are formalised, keeping them clearly in the realm of fantasy. In more dangerous scenarios, such as bondage and S/M, very clear rules are agreed, such as the 'safe word' by which the 'victim' can signal a need to be released.

Much women's clothing is designed to be sexually attractive to men, of course, and is attractive to some men because it is women's clothing. Some do, in fact, become very worried that, even though they may have a girl friend, they find themselves more interested in her clothes. This may well be encouraged by the emphasis on the female image rather than the person, and the divide between male and female worlds in a sex-role divisive culture. For some, it may be a protective diversion against the difficulties of building a relationship. If the person is already married, it might be a defence against infidelity.

There was an attempt to label Dual Role Transvestism as the 'whole girl fetish', ignoring the emotional background. Based on the theories of Watson, behaviourist psychiatrists still, in some parts of the country, use aversion therapy, even though it has not been shown to be effective for more a couple of years, if at all. It seems unlikely to me that the issue for the client is merely classical, or even operant, conditioning. It is suggested that 'symptom substitution' does not occur, but does the therapist look for later episodes of depression, for instance?

Every human being has a natural urge to dress up, to enjoy experimenting with personal adornment, strange fabrics and the exploration of all the senses. This is the right of everyone, yet it is denied to many male children and adults. The ability to do so, and to experience physical sensations, is labelled feminine. But, in trying on something lacy and flimsy, they may experience the physical and emotional sensation of wearing something pretty for the first time. They may feel the silkiness of tights, or the feeling of earrings dangling. What, for women, is an everyday experience, is entirely new to the man. The psychological arousal translates into erotic feelings.

Fetishism seems to be no problem for women, because nobody thinks anything of it. It is something that can be expressed in the open. No-one could reasonably suggest that a fifteen-inch mini-skirt is practical or even comfortable. A woman will say she wears it because she feels nice. This is, in fact, a fetish, even if it isn't immediately erotic. Where is the boundary between feeling nice and feeling sexy?

Sexual Orientation

Another concern for many is that they fear a confusion with homosexuality. There is also a general confusion too between emotional partnerships and same sex erotic interludes. The people you like to make love to must, in the end, be based on the relationships you feel comfortable with, and past emotional experiences must have their influence. What is forgotten is that it is the sort of relationship that different people need that is important, not what happens to turn them on. Gay men are in no doubt they are men, looking for other men as sexual partners. In fact they emphasise their masculine image, in contrast to heterosexual men, whose attractiveness to women is based on status.

Gay cross-dressers are most visible, of course, as drag artists. Such gay men with a feminine demeanour, labelled as 'camp', are frequently teased, even ridiculed. Referred to as 'queens' they are an underclass, paralleling the genders in heterosexual society. Lee Brewster, in an issue of *Tapestry* pointed out how their central role in Stonewall was being written out of gay history.

It is clearly over simplistic to suggest that transvestism (or transsexualism) is simply a way of avoiding the stigma of homosexuality, or that it is due to feelings of bisexuality. In fact, many people cross-dress for years with the idea of sex with another man never entering their heads.

Is it a neurosis?

Often the issue of schizophrenia is brought up in connection with transvestism. This is because of the nature of misconceptions about the former. Schizophrenia is a psychosis; it is a mental disorder, thought to have a medical basis, though it is probable that there may be inherited and environmental factors that are involved. It is characterised by disordered perceptions and thought processes that are extremely frightening and distressing to the person and those around him, or her. It does not usually take the form of an organised role, though some people have talked about cross-gender feelings in conjunction with it.

The correct condition to consider is Multiple Personality Disorder, a neurosis that involves the person switching between different personalities, often to handle different life situations. One of the most famous of these is portrayed in the book *The Three Faces of Eve*. The significant difference is that, while living in one personality, the person does not tend to be aware of the others. Transvestites are quite aware of portraying two different gender personas.

Back in the fifties, newspaper reports would sometimes feature transvestites appearing in court and insisting that they could not remember what they had been doing. At the time, I thought that it was simply an excuse, but now I am not so sure. Due to the activities of the Beaumont Society and other groups, the thought that one might be a transvestite is not so threatening as it was then.

In addition, people have become much more tolerant of unusual behaviour, thanks to the pop world, the gay communities and a general increase in acceptance of gender bending, especially by women. It occurs to me, therefore, that the guilt, in those days, could indeed have been such as to force the person into neurosis.

The two other issues that tend to be brought up are the idea of transvestism as an addiction or an obsessive compulsive disorder. In the closet, a whole range of feelings comes to the surface. One might suggest that many of them could be experienced as a man. However, the person has been taught, since his earliest childhood, that they are women's feelings; therefore, he can only experience them in the guise of a woman.

This is the fallacy of aversion therapy. If the person's transvestism is due to pressures preventing him from expressing himself as he has a right to, as a person, then the therapist is merely colluding with such pressures.

The Transvestite

It will be clear by now that transvestism is not a simple phenomenon. A range of psychological processes may be at work in different people at different times. Clearly, if therapy were to be offered, it would have to be person-centred.

The one distinguishing feature of the Dual Role Transvestite is that, as the psychological arousal reduces with familiarity, he will continue sessions of cross-dressing, without needing to go further in his sexual script. It would be easy to attribute this to negative feelings about sex and masturbation, but there is more to it than that. Such a transvestite remains content to simply experience the feelings and sensations of wearing different clothes and ornamentation, make up and experimentation with his image.

In "My Husband Wears My Clothes", Peggy Rudd tells the story of a man who led a field hospital in Korea. Every evening, the nurses would get together to relax and he found himself joining them. After a while they took pity on him, wearing his stiff uniform, and offered him a wrap to wear, and from then on they would relax together off-duty in friendly chat and comradeship. This, he said marked the start of his later cross-dressing. It seemed to me like a transvestite's fantasy, but it illustrates a point.

Many transvestites go through a period when they wish that they could find a group of female friends, without sexual feelings getting in the way. From this, it is a short step to wanting to become a part of female society. Identifying with women is very different from identifying oneself *as* a woman, however, transvestism may be unique in that, unlike many scenarios which revolve around exploration of power, there is an urge for a relationship of equality. Thus a couple will in all truth, speak of being 'best friends'. In a sense, this group of transvestites may be calling a truce in the battle of the sexes.

Moreover for those who have been social isolates during childhood, it may be a wish to find a peer group with whom they feel comfortable.

One wife complained, "She's so relaxed when she's dressed up. I wish I knew how she does it."

Clearly when the transvestite is indulging in spot of cross dressing, he is doing nothing else, but is there a deeper reason? The image put before the media is that it is a form of relaxation, but why? Also, why is it so relaxing for men but not women? A sociobiologist might suggest that it is a way of dropping out of the male dominance hierarchy.

Writers, like Krafft-Ebing and Havelock Ellis, labelled transvestism as autoerotic narcissistic fetishism, while Blanchard, in America, has coined the word 'autogynephilia', which he defines as the love, implying sexual arousal, of one's image or self, as a woman.

It seems to be a crude way of distinguishing such transsexuals and transvestites, from those who are aroused by men, as psychiatrists believe they should be. It betrays the psychiatric obsession with sexual preference as the primary issue, rather than identity, one's sense of self. It also seems an unnecessary categorisation, since those who are androphilic should find a partner without too much difficulty, while those who are gynephilic generally have to make do with themselves.

The picture of the lonely transvestite, dressing in front of a mirror, experimenting with an alternative 'self,' ignores the point that his reflection is his only source of feedback, usually, but not always, approving. Perhaps the need for wider approval is part of what brings the transvestite out of the closet.

A preoccupation with self can, of course, lead to attention seeking episodes, such as exhibitionism. There are, of course, socially acceptable ways of being exhibitionistic, like becoming a film or music hall star, but everybody has the need, from time to time, to shout, "Look! I'm here. This is me. I'm not some pale shadow." Or it can be a need for love, or approval.

Generally, it does not reach these proportions, but it often leads wives to complain of their partner's selfishness, or that their husbands spend excessive amounts of time, preening, and looking at themselves in the mirror. Being used to having the opportunity to dress up, they cannot understand what all the fuss is about.

Fantasy and Reality

Most transvestites don't identify themselves as female, but are recognising common attributes that in the man are denied expression. The feelings that are evoked, contrast with a male life that may well be very humdrum and boring. It is usual to dress as someone, and so there could be an element of identification with an admired, or loved person. Sometimes the TV will attach to a particular person's clothes, or those from a certain period, sometimes the symbol of that person, sometimes taking her as a role model. This can produce a great deal of confusion, especially if a growing number of 'female' attributes are attached and a growing number of 'male' ones are rejected. It is hardly surprising if they grow into an alternative female self, initially a fantasy, then becoming more and more real. From being an alternative schema it may become the more desirable one. The TV may feel "If I were a woman, I could have these feelings all the time and no one would mind", forgetting that women don't have such feelings all the time and that their lives can also be very humdrum and boring. Cross-dressing involves the whole person; often the person will not be doing the everyday household chores, or his ordinary daily work. Many may feel they have left their male world, but they neglect to realise that they have not really entered the female one. They are in a limbo, where they have discarded the worries of their male life, but not taken on the worries of a female life, which are not likely to be much different.

Identification

Freud has had a very bad press in recent years, particularly in the way his writing has been misconstrued by some therapists. His specific mechanisms such as the Oedipus Complex have now been largely discarded, which has tended to obscure his underlying theory of defence mechanisms, which have never been equalled.

Among these is the idea of incorporation, generally thought of as a defence against fear of an aggressor. Bettelheim, who spent some time in a concentration camp, observed that certain prisoners set out to become like their guards, a phenomenon which has been observed since, in prisons and hostage situations. What Freud actually suggested was that the fear produced strong emotions that were threatening the balance of the person's psyche – using a more modern term, one's mental homeostasis. Could not one suggest that extremely pleasurable emotions, unresolved over a period, could have a similar effect?

But many have periods of jealousy of a woman's femininity. They will see a pretty girl and say "I wish I had legs like those." Breasts are the social marker of the female image, which provides a good market among TVs of overpriced prostheses. We may picture an older man who may be strongly attracted sexually to women, but also feels great empathy with what he sees as their persona. By adopting that persona, he 'becomes' a woman.

Though many TV's are sexually very potent in their male role and, sometimes, in their female role also, most say that they feel very relaxed. Many do not, while they are dressed, feel that they are sexual at all. Besides taking a rest from their male selves, they can also escape their male sexual urges, in what is clearly a heterosexual phenomenon.

Many TV's, when they meet a girl and fall in love, say that the cross-dressing urge has gone away and they don't expect it to return.

In the first flush of romance, the need for the defence has disappeared. Thus, so many do not reveal themselves until some time in the marriage, often by being caught *in flagrante*.

But Freud made it clear that incorporation is closely associated with identification, whereby such features are not merely incorporated as part of one's persona, but internalised into an existing whole sense of self as a woman. It is an issue within himself that the person thinking he may be transsexual should consider carefully.

Books mentioned in this chapter

Reiss.I.L, (1990) *An End to Shame: Shaping our next sexual revolution,* New York: Prometheus Books.

Rudd, P.,(1990, 2003) *My Husband Wears My Clothes,* PM Publishers (USA)

Saypen, A., (1995) *A Little Bit Of Our History: An Interview with Lee Brewster,* from *Tapestry,* Issue 70, Winter 95, Massachusetts: International Foundation for Gender Education

The Academic View of Transvestism
Jed Bland

Historically, in this country, there seems to be three strands to cross-dressing. In the Middle Ages, young boys were used to take female parts in the theatre. Cross dressing was also common in pageants, festivals and carnivals – a hangover, it is thought, from pagan rituals. From the sixteenth and into the nineteenth century, increasing social unrest brought riots involving cross dressing, such as the Rebecca Riots and, in Ireland, the Molly McGuires. Just why cross-dressing was involved is a matter for debate, but at the very least, it was an expression of rebellion against the social order.

Hostility to any sort of infringement of sexual and gender boundaries first began to appear with Puritan attitudes in seventeenth century. Thus the third strand is the eighteenth century 'Molly' clubs, which, it has been suggested, were the means by which homosexuality, in emerging as a distinct sub-culture, announced itself. Romanticism, in the nineteenth century, provided a tension between the view of women as delicate fragile beings and men as coarse brutes, and a model of self-reliant womanliness and gentle manliness. The fear arose that any hint of demasculinisation might lead to homosexuality, and dressing as a woman by a man would encourage both.

Thus there are elements both of social unrest and cultural psychology. Many writers suggest that, as the Church became less influential, first the judiciary, then science was turned to as an instrument of social control. As the courts dealt with more and more activities that became proscribed, they turned to the medical profession to provide definitions they could work with. Furthermore, an increasing number of people who were marginalised by their behaviour, turned to the medical profession in the hope of a sympathetic means of resolving their difficulty.

Richard von Krafft-Ebing categorised many of the differing expressions of sexuality, culminating with the publication of his *Psychopathia Sexualis,* which did not, in fact, include transvestism *per se*, though he did include cases of what he called "dress fetishism". His belief was in line with those of the Church, since the beginning of the millennium, that any activities that were not strictly directed at procreation were "perversions of the sexual instinct."

In the mid-nineteenth century, Karl Ulrichs was among the first to publicly proclaim himself as homosexual. He wrote of *"men . . . . who might be described as of feminine soul enclosed in a male body,"* and of *"women whose definition would be just the reverse."* Half a century or more before the group *Mermaids* was formed, in an early feminist publication *Love's Coming of Age,* Edward Carpenter wrote *"But we may point out how hard it is, especially for the young among them, that a veil of complete silence should be drawn over the subject, leading to the most painful misunderstandings, and perversions and confusions of mind . . . ."*

Towards the end of the nineteenth century, three writers, Havelock Ellis, Freud and Hirschfeld, were instrumental in modifying beliefs about sexual behaviours which, up to that time, had been associated with ideas about degeneracy and hereditary taint. Hirschfeld, in 1910, published some sixteen case studies, observing that most of them were heterosexual. He disengaged transvestism from eroticism by proposing his "Theory of Sexual Intermediaries." He listed four determinants of sexual role: sexual organs, physical characteristics, sex drive and the other emotional characteristics. It was not until forty years later, that Benjamin defined gender and gender identity, publishing *The Transsexual Phenomenon* in 1966.

Meanwhile, in *Three Essays on Sexuality*, Freud had implicated early developmental issues in later sexual behaviour, though he always maintained that biological factors would one day be found. Havelock Ellis, influenced by Freud, was interested in the relationship between sexual practices and cultural norms. He concentrated on the sex roles of his subjects rather than what they wore, and being uncomfortable with the word transvestite, coined the term *sexo-aesthetic inversion,* but, since inversion was associated with homosexuality, changed it to *eonism*. In that his work dealt with erotic behaviour – what Money would later call paraphilias – his work led on to that by Kinsey, though the latter did not include transvestism in his studies. Thus began the conceptual dichotomy between sexuality and gender which persists to this day.

In the thirties, there was a reaction against psychoanalysis, with the movement to establish psychology as a 'true' science with rigorously tested theories. The central theme of psychology, therefore, became that only events that can be observed and precisely measured can be admitted to the theory, in other words overt behaviours and external evidence of thought processes. It excludes the internal processes of psychoanalysis and any inborn abilities or mental processes. The work of Pavlov and the idea of conditioned responses arising from specific stimuli, suggested that behaviour could be modified by reward – or punishment. With transvestism firmly labelled as a pathology, it led to aversion therapy and other more stringent practices.

The forerunners of the modern self-help movement came in the late twentieth century self-advocacy by transvestites, such as Virginia Prince in America, who began a group called the Foundation for Full Personality Expression, which later became The Society for the Second Self. A European chapter of the FPE appeared, followed in 1966 in England by the Beaumont Society. The story goes that, at the first meeting, there were twelve attending, plus a dog. The dog was made an honorary member since, it was said, he often felt he was a cat. The Beaumont Trust was formed shortly afterwards.

It has to be said that there is little in the modern literature about transvestites, since they rarely visit clinics. Most, nowadays, simply want to be left alone to enjoy themselves. Those who need help with sorting out emotional or relationship issues turn to the self-help groups, or semi-professional helplines like that of the Beaumont Trust. The first field study since Hirschfeld was probably that by Brierley in 1979, *Transvestites: A Handbook with Case Studies,* in which he highlighted the cross-gender identity which some individuals experience, that is, they speak of an alternative feminine self.

Is there, then, a situation where this alternative self becomes the more important one, the more real? This is the scenario that wives, perhaps, fear most, when they discover the source of their husband's preoccupation. It may be why transvestites distinguish themselves from transsexuals, and why, perhaps, they insist that their cross-dressing is the issue, rather than any inner feelings they may have.

The last thirty years has seen an increasing amount of sociological literature. Ekins' *Male Femaling*, in particular, set out to analyse transgender presentation as a spectrum of processes, rather than a list of people labels. He describes a career in terms of three modes: 'body femaling' in which they change their appearance or their bodily characteristics, 'erotic' femaling where the experience is erotic, deliberately or otherwise, and may involve a more or less complex script, and 'gender femaling' where the behaviours and emotions of the opposite sex may be adopted. The first stage may be 'beginning femaling' which may be followed by strategies of concealment, with the resulting stress, and by 'fantasy femaling'.

The person moves on to 'doing femaling' which at first may be solitary, that is in total secrecy, and may remain so, or solo in public, where the person may either seek to make a statement of some kind, or may make as much effort as possible to 'pass' unnoticed. Grayson Perry, the artist and potter, in an interview for the Gender Trust magazine, said *"I wore fashionable clothes and walked about with no hassle . . . . Then I started to think 'this is not doing it for me.' I was trying to get attention and not getting it"*

This is associated with 'dyadic doing' brought about by the sheer need for human company, the need to share. It may be within the home with a tolerant spouse, or in establishments specialising in cross-dressing, or in looking for companions outside of everyday life, and latterly, virtual cyber-companions through the Internet.

With the stigma placed on exhibitionism, let alone eroticism, and the need to avoid it, the next stage 'constituting femaling' becomes crucial as the person, as Ekins puts it, gives "much thought and consideration to 'finding the label that fits'" and "Having adopted a label, meanings can now be ordered and understood."

With passing time and experience, a stage is reached where the person has a clear view of where he is at, and how he should build a stable role. Ekins calls this 'consolidation' - in effect, everyone goes through their own 'real life experience', whatever role they do it in.

In general the possibilities are: 'aparting', where a strong boundary is constructed between the male and female worlds, 'substituting' in which the male world is discarded in favour of the female one, and 'integrating' which is performed by those who seek to discard the constraints of sex-role stereotypes.

Some transsexual people may be upset by this picture which seems to merge all the different categories into one process. What Ekins is saying, however, is that, because of their innate temperament, life experience or whatever, they may have moved quickly to the substituting stage, while, for instance, very young gender dysphoric children may not have thought about concealment. Being transsexual or a cross-dresser are two possible endpoints of 'gender dysphoria' when an individual has gained his, or her, own gender identity/role.

Gender clinics are, or should be, for people who are gender dysphoric in any way, not merely those who are transsexual. It explains why a large proportion of clients do not go on to full reassignment. The aim, after all, is not to 'change them over, come what may,' but to help them attain a stable and enduring quality of life. There is a note of caution here. The confidentiality of the client is paramount. Too often, a wife complains that she has found that her husband has been seeing a psychiatrist in secret. Even though the client may be uncertain about himself, he owes it to his wife to discuss his feelings with her. It may, of course, be that he thinks his wife will prefer the idea of his being 'diagnosed' as 'transsexual' which can be portrayed as a 'condition', than of him being transvestite, which is seen as a choice.

Books Mentioned In This Chapter
Richard Ekins (1997) *Male femaling: A grounded theory approach to Cross-dressing and Sex-changing,* Routledge
An Interview With Grayson Perry, GT News, Spring 2004, The Gender Trust.

Getting Referred
Dr. Russell Reid

Decide whether you want to go Private or through the NHS.

To go Private, discuss with your G.P. or TS self-help group or Internet chat-line the Gender Psychiatrist who best meets your particular needs. Before committing yourself, however, you may feel it necessary to explore and try to understand your situation and motives with some in-depth discussion with a counsellor or psychotherapist (there's not much difference these days). Obviously your counsellor, therapist and in due course, your psychiatrist must be knowledgeable about GID.

Arrange to consult a psychiatrist who is up to date with the latest treatment options and is prepared to prescribe and monitor your hormones, liaise with your G.P. and guide and facilitate the process at your own pace without being overly enthusiastic nor unnecessarily obstructive. The psychiatrist will want to discuss your background, history and life-experiences including relationships with partners of either sex. He, or she, will want to make sure you understand what you are letting yourself into if you decide you are Transsexual and want to transition. Before this, however, your psychiatrist will want to exclude mental illness and severe personality disorder along with other conditions mimicking Transsexualism such as Fetishistic Transvestism or Drag-Queenism or even - currently fashionable in the USA - Multiple Personality Disorder or Aspergers Syndrome.

To go through the NHS, visit your GP who may try and talk you out of it. Insist on being referred to your local NHS Psychiatrist who will or should agree to a "tertiary referral" to a Gender Clinic near where you live. This may take some time since NHS funding needs to be agreed by the Health

Authority or Primary Care Trust (PCT). In most of southern England this will be Charing Cross GIC, in London. There are, or were, other GIC's in Leeds at St James Hospital, Leicester at Leicester General Infirmary, and in Newcastle at The Royal Victoria Infirmary. Expect a wait of anything from 6 months to 18 years (if you live in Sheffield).

If you opt for the NHS route, don't expect anything to happen quickly. You will be seen by 2 different psychiatrists 3 months apart, and will need to have changed Gender Role and have started your "Real Life Experience" before being recommended hormones. These will then be prescribed by your GP, provided of course, he agrees with the recommendation of the GIC Consultant Psychiatrists.

Culture, History and Law

Gender and Cross Dressing Across Time and Culture
Jed Bland

The Chevalier Charles, Geneviève, Louis, Auguste, André, Timothée d'Eon de Beaumont, after whom the Beaumont Trust (and the Beaumont Society) is named, was born in 1728 to a family of lawyers in Tonnere. After graduating from college, he worked in the fiscal department of Paris, then as a royal censor of books. In 1756 he became a spy for King Louis XV, who sent him on a secret mission to Russia to meet Empress Elizabeth I. He travelled as a secretary to the Chevalier Douglas, and disguised himself as a woman in order to meet Elizabeth in secret. In 1762, he was appointed a captain of the Dragoons and served with courage. In recognition of his services, he was awarded the Cross of Saint-Louis, a rare honour which gave him the title Chevalier d'Eon.

The following year, he was sent to London as Plenipotentiary Minister, while spying for King Louis for a possible invasion. He quarelled with the French ambassador, the Comte de Guerchy, and was recalled. Being reluctant to give up a lavish lifestyle, he refused to leave England and, in 1764, published his memoires including correspondence dealing with his recall. In 1766 Louis XV granted him an annual pension of 12,000 livres. Here the story becomes a mite confused, indeed, there are substantial differences in every account you read. Some suggest that d'Eon insisted that he should be recognised as a woman, and that the King gave him an official order to wear women's clothes, even providing funds for his female wardrobe.

However, he was clearly spending some of his time as a man, for in 1768 he was initiated as a Freemason. Their records deny that he had ever worn women's clothes before this time, even though he wrote in his memoirs of cross-dressing in childhood. He was not seen as effeminate and, on occasion wore the uniform of a French Dragoon captain, yet rumours began to spread that he actually was a woman. Finally, in 1777, the matter reached court. He was accused of masquerading as a man, and was ordered to revert. A witness testified to having seen her bosom, evidence of which would seem to be confirmed by a portrait painted at about that time.

After the French Revolution, d'Eon's annual pension was suspended. He had to sell many of his possessions and, to earn money, he participated in fencing tournaments. During his final years he shared his apartment with a widow, Mrs. Cole, whose husband had been an admiral. He died in London on May 21, 1810. A surgeon, who examined him, reported in the *Times* of 25, May, 1810, that he "found the male organs in every respect perfectly formed."

D'Eon Beaumont was not the only famous cross-dresser from this period. Often noted are the Lord Cornbury and the Abbé de Choisy. Lord Cornbury was Governor of New York from 1702-1708 and was extremely unpopular. There is considerable doubt about whether he did actually cross-dress, or whether it was a rumour put about by his enemies. The Abbé de Choisy, on the other hand, lived openly in one role or the other throughout his life in late 17th. Century France, and wrote his *"Memoires de l'Abbé de Choisy habillé en femme."*

It has been suggested that, if we did not have such polarized notions of what it is to be a man or a woman, we would not have transsexualism or transvestism. But there are fundamental differences that have existed from time immemorial, not just in physiology, but in men's and women's needs and agendas. Nevertheless, anthropology is showing that their expression is manifested in many different ways in different cultures.

The ladyboys of Thailand and surrounding countries have long been a feature of travellers' tales, and were usually dismissed as homosexual prostitutes, regardless of the fact that the same cultures had male rent boys. Less well known were the *fa'afa'fine* of Tahiti and Samoa, and the *mahu* of Hawa'ii. In India, there were the *hjras,* who, unlike the others, were castrated, their aim being ascetism in the service of the goddess Bukhara Mata.

Serious studies began with the multiple gender systems among almost all the Native American Indian tribes. It is clear that, although they were the teachers and keepers of tribal lore, their function was practical, helping with domestic chores where their strength might be useful. There was nothing effete about them. There is a story among the Zunis about how, when a village was raided by Navahos, while the warriors were away hunting, the *llamana* and the women together repelled them. Indeed the name of one notable *boté* of the Crow tribe, Osh-tisch, means "Finds them and kills them." He accompanied the Crow warriors, along with a female warrior, "The Other Magpie", when they assisted General George Crook at the Battle of Rosebud Creek.

It is not true, as some suggest, that these people were intersexed. The *hjras,* in particular, distinguish between 'born' and 'made'. Such gender roles are usually permanent through life. Gender switching is less well reported in the literature, and usually associated with ritual magic. Although many writers might have found the subject distasteful, it may also have been that disclosure of such secret rituals would be taboo.

The behaviours that are considered appropriate for each gender varies widely, and in often subtle ways, between one culture and another. Many writers have been confused by what they describe as the transvestite behaviour of the Wodabi people of the Sahara. Each year they hold a get-together, where the men put on make-up and stand in line, adopting formalised poses which, in fact, show off their clear eyes and healthy teeth. Though their movements appear decidedly feminine to Western eyes, they are in no way transvestites as we understand the word, for they are dressing up as men to attract female brides.

The distinction between role taking and identification may be illustrated by the *chukchi* of Siberia, who, it has been suggested, have seven gender roles. Among them, whole families will be shaman, and some men undergo a transformation referred to as "soft man being". It may begin in childhood, initially by the adoption of a feminine hairstyle, later by female dress. In time even their physical appearance and demeanour may change. It does not imply a change of sex - they may marry and have children. However there are some, referred to as "similar to a woman" who live for life as women and take husbands. Many hope that, in time, they could change the organs of their sex altogether, "which would be much more convenient."

Exploration of that unfathomable division between the sexes and the mysteries of sexuality and procreation, has been central to ritual throughout the world and throughout history. In West Africa, for instance, cross-dressing has implied access to sources of power far stronger than mere human ones. During recent troubles in Liberia, rebels were seen wearing wigs or masks, or even wedding gowns, signalling that they were in a spiritual in-between state of superhuman power. Traditional male initiation rituals involved dressing in female clothes as a symbolic passage through a dangerous indeterminate zone between male and female identity before finally becoming a man.

Transvestism, the Church and the Law
An Historical Review
Vicky (727)

Much of the prejudice that attaches to society's attitudes towards sexual minority groups and towards the type of gender dysfunction under discussion relates to religious concepts devised originally out of political or policy decisions relating to a different age and culture and having little application in current circumstances. For the prejudiced who wish to find an excuse, however, to harass minority groups quotations taken out of context from religious works often dating back three or four thousand years can provide useful ammunition.

Much of the present secular legal policy in Western European and American civilisations, therefore, (and this does not apply to Buddhist or Taoist philosophies) is based on these early ecclesiastical laws. The failure to condemn such bigotry provides to the author's mind the unacceptable face of current religious attitude.

With regard to homosexuality, however, there is certainly evidence that the church is now inclined to pursue charity rather more than pure dogma. To change public attitudes, however, requires more than mere acceptance. It requires a positive will to seek out on behalf of the oppressed.

The church's case against cross-dressing rests on an obscure paragraph in Chapter XXII of the Book of Deuteronomy. Here, under Jewish law, some 3,000 years ago, the practice was frowned upon. Verse 5 states as follows: *"A woman shall not wear that which pertaineth unto a man, neither shall a man put on a woman's garment. For whosoever doeth these things is an abomination unto the Lord thy God."*

It is worth noting that the first part of that paragraph has been ignored by many women in and out of church for a long time. Thus the argument can only be used against the male transvestite when quoted alone and out of context. It is also worth noting that in biblical Palestine the male raiment as in Arab countries today was much more like a long dress than like trousers. Indeed many Muslim women now wear trousers in order to cover their legs so that in terms of the type of garment appropriate to the sexes there has been a role reversal!

To apply such an argument, therefore, to contemporary Western society is plainly fatuous. If one looks at other parts of the same chapter in Deuteronomy then we find for example: *"Thou shalt not plough with an ox and an ass together."* *"Thou shalt not wear a mingled stuff wool and linen together."* *"Thou shalt not make thee fringes upon the four borders of thy vesture wherewith thou coverest thyself."*

Later in the chapter commencing at Verse 13, advice is given on what to do with unfaithful partners. If a man accuses his wife of not being a virgin at marriage then the matter has to be taken before the elders and the woman's father must bring tokens of his daughter's virginity, namely the blood-stained sheets after the first night. If it can be proved that the husband is lying and the girl was a virgin then the man is to be taken and chastised and has to pay the father a hundred shekels of silver.

On the other hand: *"But if this thing be true that the tokens of virginity were not found in the damsel then they shall bring out the damsel to the door of her father's house and the men of the city shall stone her with stones that she die."*

In Verse 22: *"If a man be found lying with a woman married to an husband then they shall both of them die. The man that lay with the woman and the woman."*

It will be seen gratefully that we are somewhat selective in the application we make of the ancient Judaic law. Perhaps mercifully we only choose these days to apply selective rules to the behaviour of our contemporaries. Lest it be thought that these are matters no longer relevant, however, we must remember that much of the Muslim religious code and that of the Christians is based upon ancient Judaic law which itself was part of a monotheistic concept that grew up in pre-Christian Palestine and is still applied in some of the stricter Muslim countries. We have seen currently in Iran barbaric punishments being meted out for those who offend the religious code, and at the time of writing of this book it was reported in The Daily Telegraph that two men aged 24 and 30 had been executed by firing squad in the central Iranian city of Shiraz for committing homosexual acts.

Indeed, most of the ecclesiastical laws relating to sexuality were originally formulated by the Jews as a means of maintaining their own religious and racial purity when competing with pagan religions in ancient Palestine. Homosexuality was condemned more because of its association with religious practises of other faiths at the time. Even masturbation which is now recognised as a harmless pursuit, which brings relief of sexual tension to those without other outlets, was condemned as sinful again on the doubtful basis of somebody who actually practised *coitus interruptus* and is the theme of a little morality story in Genesis Chapter 38.

In verse 6 it tells us that Judah took a wife for Er, his first born and her name was Tamar. Er, Judah's first born, was wicked in the sight of the Lord and the Lord slew him.

"And Judah said unto Onan 'Go in unto thy brother's wife and perform the duty of an husband's brother unto her and raise up the seed to thy brother'."

"And Onan knew that the seed should not be his and it came to pass when he went in unto his brother's wife that he spilled it on the ground lest he should give seed to his brother. And the thing which he did was evil in the sight of the Lord and he slew him also." There was little charity in Old Testament justice, particularly when meted out by the deity, but the point of the story was that Onan did not wish to get his brother's widow pregnant. Masturbation, as such, was hardly the point of the exercise, yet the word onanism, synonymous with masturbation, is derived from this brief tale.

Much of the prejudice directed against the transvestite has been the result of the misconception that there is a direct link with homosexuality. We should look, therefore, at why homosexuality has been the recipient of so much ill-informed prejudice.

Much of it is owed to St. Paul's comments as found in his epistle to the Romans Chapter I. St. Paul is here commenting on how man has given up Godly pursuits and has instead chosen to worship the fleshly pursuits of lower creatures: *"They have given themselves up to vile passions and behave in an ungodly manner."*

In Verse 26 he states: *"For though women change the natural use into that which is against nature and likewise also the men leaving the natural use of the woman found in their lust one toward another, men with men working unseemliness and receiving in themselves that recompense of their error which was due."*

Later in the chapter it is clear that St. Paul is referring to all types of sinfulness and not specifically to homosexuality, and indeed female homosexuality is again mentioned before that of the male, though in Britain lesbianism has never been specifically an offence on the civil code of law though male homosexuality has and, in some instances, still is. Nevertheless, these quotations are often used along with the famous story of the destruction of Sodom, as justification for the persecution of homosexual minority groups.

While the Church's attitude has recently become more tolerant it is still fair to say that the official viewpoint is that those who are aware that they are homosexual should abstain from all sexual activity throughout their lives and the church will exercise charity against their state of mind but does not approve of any physical expression arising therefrom. The same of course applies to heterosexual activity outside of wedlock. It is as recently, however, as 1953 that the then Archbishop of Canterbury, Dr. Fisher, is quoted as saying: "Let it be understood that homosexual indulgence is a shameful vice and a grievous sin from which deliverance is to be sought by every means."

More recently, however, various church bodies have been considering the church's attitude to sexuality in, for instance, a report entitled *A Christian Understanding of Human Sexuality* prepared for the Methodists and arising from a 1976 report to conference by the Division of Social Responsibility and the Faith and Order Committee. This was accepted by the Methodist conference in 1979.

The report is concerned mainly with general issues with regard to the relationship between sexuality and Christian thinking. It emphasises that the Christian ideal of love is one in which the beloved finds fulfilment and that there must be a mutuality between those involved. Physical sexuality should be an expression of this love between two people and is sanctified by marriage. They take as their starting point that the whole of scripture is God's written word which is believed to be wholly trustworthy and self consistent. Admittedly, many modern biblical scholars would feel that some Jewish writing included in the current collection of books that go to make up the Bible may be of somewhat doubtful validity, certainly in terms of their deistic origin but one must accept that this is the Christian philosophy but equally of course, that there are many people who do not accept this as a basis for contemporary morality.

In their comments on Section B of the report the conference looked at deviations: *"The presence of a norm indicates the possibility of deviations from the norm and so it is with marriage. Those categorically condemned in scripture include fornication, adultery, prostitution, incest and rape, and the biblical quotations from which this opinion is founded are given in this report."*

Section C deals with the Methodist church's attitude to homosexuality and the report distinguishes clearly between homosexuality and transsexualism and transvestism, defining these terms. In paragraph C11 they state: *"it has frankly to be recognised that the biblical evidence is scarce and the Old Testament passages highly specific. It is hazardous to create general and universal principles out of the few prohibitions contained in the Bible and questions must be asked about the validity of the mosaic law in the Christian era."* It later comments that while homosexual people deserve sympathy and compassion nonetheless homosexual acts are intrinsically disordered and can in no case be approved of.

The Sodom story is contained in Genesis Chapter 19, Verses 1-26. Anal intercourse is, however, never spelt out as the sin which the Sodomites had practised although it has become a term used for such practice between homosexuals in current times. The real sin, however, would seem to have been the violence and would-be rape which the inhabitants sought to perpetrate against visitors to the city, though the host's offer of his daughter as an alternative confirms the sexual element. Indeed, in Jude VII where the prophet refers to strange flesh after which the men of Sodom lusted, it is possible that this term could mean angels rather than other men. Other denunciations of homosexual activity in the rest of the Bible do not link the practice with the Sodom story. The display of divine wrath in the Sodom story, however, is linked with general wickedness which happened to include possibly homosexual activity. Furthermore, it appears that the general male population was attempting to act in a perverted way, though presumably were capable at other times of heterosexual activity.

Other references in the Old Testament refer to male cult prostitutes, which practices were frequent in other religions at the time. These references are found in Deuteronomy Chapter XXIII, Verse 17; I Kings, Chapter XV, Verse 12; Chapter XXII, Verse 46 and II Kings, Chapter XXIII, Verse 7. The Qadesh had a homosexual function, though was part of a general fertility cult. The comments in Deuteronomy, Chapter VII, Verses 1-6 would seem to refer to this aspect.

Leviticus, Chapter XVIII, Verse 22 and Chapter XX, Verse 13 are more specific in condemning male homosexual acts, the latter requiring the death penalty for them. A similar ban is put on incest and bestiality. However, the preservation of the state of Israel at that time seemed to require a large number of commands, the moral force of which is hard to see today. The same legal code that requires the death of a homosexual person, also bans eating meat with blood in it, sexual intercourse during menstruation, the crossbreeding of cattle, wearing garments made of two kinds of fabric, certain hairstyles and tattoo marks, all of which are acceptable today.

There is no reference specifically to homosexuality in the gospels. However, without exception, biblical references to homosexual acts are prohibitive and condemnatory and it would be imprudent to assume that the biblical evidence allows us to shift an undue measure of reprehensibility away from homosexual acts. Thus the church continues to be unhappy about homosexuality and condemns its practice for those who wish to live by the Christian faith.

While many of those who are prejudiced would not call themselves Christians, it is unfortunately the case that the lead taken by authority can often be used unscrupulously by those who want an excuse.

Furthermore, medieval ecclesiastical law has a great influence on the development of secular laws. Under ecclesiastical law in Britain, the death penalty was invoked for homosexual practices and various other "deviancies". During Henry VIII's reign, in 1533, a secular law was introduced punishing sodomy, that is anal intercourse, by death and this was only revoked in 1861 when the maximum penalty became life imprisonment. In 1885 an offence of gross indecency was created which included many potentially male homosexual activities other than anal intercourse.

It was only in 1967 when Leo Abse's law was passed through Parliament that homosexuality between consenting male adults in private became legal. So far as the British Isles is concerned homosexuality remains illegal if one party is not consenting or is under the age of valid consent. An adult by this definition was anyone over twenty-one (now eighteen), and thus homosexuality is illegal when under the age of eighteen, despite the fact that such behaviour is often a normal phase of adolescence and male sexual urges tend to be at their strongest around 18 or 19. Homosexuality, at the time of writing, remains illegal for members of Her Majesty's armed services, and for merchant seamen when on board ship.

The definition of "in private" has been the subject of some case law. Basically, it is not private if more than two people are present, nor if the act takes place in an area to which the public have access. This includes, therefore, a parked car on the highway, a public lavatory, and conceivably even an hotel bedroom. There are still, therefore, many pitfalls.

The law in this regard varies very much from country to country in Western Europe, some being much more tolerant than others. The law varies from one state to another in the United States of America. In general, those countries with a Muslim or Christian or Jewish tradition tend to be restrictive.

Some Western European countries such as Denmark and Holland now have much more enlightened legal attitudes towards sexual minority groups and Asian countries, on the whole, see little need to apply legal sanctions to such personal moral matters.

We have dealt at some length on the ecclesiastical and secular laws with regard to homosexuality because herein lies the background to much prejudice with regard to transvestism, since as we have noted it is a popular misconception that transvestism is equated with homosexual behaviour.

While it is in fact perfectly legal to go in public dressed in whatever way one wishes subject to not offending public decency, the breach of the peace laws are sometimes invoked if the police choose to arrest such individuals. Thus the Telegraph reported in 1977 that a youth of 19 had breached public decorum by appearing in drag in public and was sentenced to three months detention at Dunfermline Sherriff's Court. The youth admitted three charges of breach of the peace, public order and decorum by wearing female clothes in Cowdenbeath public park, at a refuse tip and in a Dunfermline street.

Another report, in the Daily Telegraph, a paper which used not to sink too far into the depths of sensationalism was published on November 29th, 1979 under the headline of "Husband Wore Bra and Two Nightgowns".

A man accused of murdering another man seemingly excused himself largely on the basis that his victim cross dressed. He told detectives how he bludgeoned his lover's transvestite husband to death with a spade to win her freedom. He and the man's wife had long discussions over what to do because the husband refused to give her a divorce and the wife wished to escape her unhappy third marriage.

"We talked as to how we could then carry out the rest of our actions so that she could obtain her release from the intolerable surroundings."

The wife had shown her boyfriend what her husband was wearing under his normal clothes, while he was asleep. "Much to my horror and disgust he had on two nightdresses, one orange and one blue, and under this he was wearing an all-in-one foundation garment which was padded at the breast. He was also wearing a pair of women's tights."

The barrister produced in court what the wife had described as her husband's dressing up box.

The police made a search of the victim's private possessions and "This revealed a number of sex magazines. One was called Forum and had an article on cross-dressing in Australia. The police also found two pairs of tights which the wife claimed belonged to her husband."

A number of factors emerged from this report which illustrates our theme. One would think it more appropriate to search the alleged murderer's private possessions than the victim's. Furthermore, it is hard to see the relevance of some of these facts to the case which was that a lover had murdered his girlfriend's husband. Were the defence suggesting that owning tights and a copy of Forum was in some way a mitigating feature in terms of the defendant's actions?

It is also curious that the Daily Telegraph reporter chose to dwell at some length on these particular irrelevancies, presumably considering them more newsworthy than the real issues in the case.

Brierley in his book *Transvestism: A Handbook with Case Studies,* comments that different countries have widely different attitudes towards the use of the law for the prosecution of transvestites.

"It appears that both Denmark and Holland have laws which are specifically relevant to the transvestite and yet they are amongst the most tolerant countries. England has no law specifically prohibiting transvestism. Much of the most commonly used law in prosecutions is the common law offence of behaviour liable to cause a breach of the peace."

The Queen's peace is defined as a normal state of society and any interruption of that peace and good order which ought to prevail in a civilised country is a breach of that peace. This is of course extraordinarily vague and the law does not insist that the offender is causing a breach of the peace, only that he is judged likely to. Should a complaint be made by a member of the public, therefore, there is little doubt that the prosecution would be successful even if the witness was in no way upset or disturbed by their observation.

Brierley quotes a case where a transvestite, minding his own business, was walking through a town and was set upon by a gang of youths. The gang who created the disturbance were not prosecuted but the transvestite was prosecuted, apparently because he was regarded as having provoked the youths by his behaviour.

One transvestite has been prosecuted when found sitting in his car in the early hours of the morning simply because the parked car appeared to raise the suspicions of the police who, when they found the state of the occupant, decided to press charges. As Brierley points out the outcome of such prosecutions are minimal so far as the conviction itself is concerned but may be personally devastating since many of the offenders can lose their careers, possibly their families and become the butt of newspaper voyeurism.

Another offence on the statute book is that of "conduct likely to insult a female". This may be invoked if a male transvestite needs to use a public toilet and enters the ladies toilet. Of course, should he enter the male toilet while cross-dressed he is more than likely to be had up for suspected importuning, so that in the absence of unisex toilets in this country the transvestite presumably is required not to have a bladder.

Even when not using the toilet the transvestite may be accused of soliciting or importuning. Not infrequently the transvestite taking hesitant first steps outdoors, when inexperienced, may choose a quiet road in the late evening. Often he has no particular place to go and is just enjoying a sense of new-found freedom. His behaviour may, however, look somewhat suspicious and may call attention to himself from passers-by, particularly the police, who may suspect him of prostitution.

Brierley states that the evidence for such an offence may need to be very nebulous. Stone's Justices manual used to cite possession of a powder puff as acceptable evidence that a homosexual act had taken place! Radzinowicz in 1957 quoted artificial reddening of the lips and face as acceptable evidence of importuning. Smiling at another person, particularly in a public lavatory or the length of time spent there may be crucial evidence for the prosecution.

An old law which may be invoked is the Public Order Act of 1936. This was originally concerned with the disorder of public marches and the violent demonstrations of fascists in the pre-war days. It has been utilised subsequently, however, in widely differing circumstances.

Briefly, an offence has been committed if there is a visible representation which is threatening, abusive or insulting with intent to provoke a breach of the peace or whereby a breach of the peace is likely to be occasioned.

There are also byelaws in some cities, and provisions within the Metropolitan Police Act of 1839, which can also be invoked locally to prosecute a transvestite who, while he may only be bound over, may suffer the result of newspaper publicity. Furthermore, the police in the course of their inquiries may decide to visit the individual's home and the revelation that a father perhaps is at the police station dressed in women's clothing can be a matter of considerable trauma to a family who perhaps for very good reasons had been kept in the dark about this particular element of their father's behaviour. Some policemen are more tactful than others.

The heterosexual transvestite may still fall foul of the law by being suspected of engaging in homosexual activities even if soliciting or importuning is not in question.

The relevant laws quoted are Section 5 of the Public Order Act 1936 under which insulting behaviour likely to cause a breach of the peace is an offence. Under the Sexual Offences Act 1956 it is illegal for a man to "persistently solicit or importune in a public place for immoral purposes". The courts appear to have accepted at times very dubious evidence on which they were prepared to convict. Cases quoted in the above-mentioned book include a man found guilty of soliciting on the grounds that when visiting a couple of lavatories he smiled at people. *(Houghton v. Mead 1913, 1 KB)* and the judge commented that it seemed not unimportant in an offence of this kind that the face and lips of the man appeared to have been artificially reddened and in his pocket a powder puff with pink powder upon it was found. It is recommended that if a transvestite is arrested on the grounds of behaviour likely to cause a breach of the peace, that through their lawyer they should try to get the police to prove who was insulted.

The police witnesses should be asked why anybody should be insulted at seeing someone in drag, unisex now being in fashion, and if arrested for going into a female toilet ask which toilet they are expected to go in. Naturally, however, most women might reasonably be insulted by the presence of a male in a public female toilet and this must be respected.

If charged with soliciting then the police must be able to show who exactly the transvestite was supposed to be soliciting and the point must be made that the law requires persistently to be soliciting which implies that a single episode would not be relevant. Evidence of heterosexuality such as the fact that one is married can often be a help.

The transvestite is recommended to carry some document signed by a responsible person such as the medical practitioner that such a person is known to be a transvestite and known to be of good character. If living full-time they should carry a copy of any statutory declaration such as a change of name and documents such as a Beaumont Society membership card. This often helps reassure the police that there has been no criminal intent. The reader should note, however, that the cases quoted relate to a time of prejudice and lack of understanding. The Police are now much more aware and sensitive and, indeed, attend courses in dealing with minorities - cross gender behaviour in particular. Further more the Human Rights laws introduced in October 2000 now make it a much safer world.

Transsexuals may run into more specific legal problems. These include such matters as the validity of marriage. The famous case quoted is that of *Corbett v. Corbett (1970 2 All ER 884)* which concerned the marriage of April Ashley who was born a male and had a sex change operation.

She subsequently married a male and, on the breakdown of this marriage, her husband asked for a decree of nullity, under the Matrimonial Causes Act, 1973 Section 11, which states that for a marriage to he valid there has to be a male and a female. The Court accepted this.

The converse of this relates to divorce where an individual who is married decides to have a sex change operation. The other party may sue for divorce on the grounds of cruelty or deprivation of conjugal rights or unreasonable behaviour. In most cases, divorce has been upheld, though a case quoted in The Daily Telegraph on the 14th November, 1958 produced a contrary opinion. Custody of children tends to go in favour of the non-transsexual partner.

Certain problems may arise with regard to employment. It has been held by the National Insurance Commissioner that the male-to-female transsexual could not claim retirement pension at 60 but only at 65. Although the retirement age for women is to be raised to 65, the rate at which contributions are paid is also affected. There may also be problems with company and personal private plans. It is also probably the case that the wife of a female-to-male transsexual would not be able to qualify for a wife's retirement pension based on the transsexual's contributions.

The Sex Discrimination Act of 1975 has been held by some to be relevant in problems associated with transvestism and transsexualism. This law is designed to prevent discrimination on grounds of sex in spheres of employment, accommodation etc. and one might reasonably suppose that it would be unlawful to discriminate against transsexuals in these areas. In the case of *White v. The British Sugar Corporation (1977 IRLR 121)* it was held that sex signified original biological sex and not present gender orientation.

Here a female-to-male transsexual had applied for a job as an electrician's mate. He was given the job, but when it was discovered that White was biologically a female this was reported to the management and he was sacked. The tribunal held that he was in law a woman and it was not relevant that the name had been changed to a man's and his unemployment benefit card and registration with the DHSS had been altered to a male name. He was not therefore discriminated against as a male.

They also stated, however, that White was not discriminated against as a woman on the basis that firstly he had deceived the management; secondly that men were justified in objecting to a woman sharing their toilets and thirdly, that the job entailed working on Sundays which under the Factories Act legislation, the woman can only do with an exemption order from the Health and Safety executive which was not in this instance the case.

It would seem that management can take into account the prejudices of other workers in dismissing someone from employment and a transsexual because he or she is employed before the operation has no guarantee therefore of continuing in employment after a sex change. Even though the law is changing in this area, the employment situation for post-operative transsexuals and even more so perhaps for pre-operative transsexuals is a difficult one. Many, therefore, remain unemployed or have to go into jobs which put them socially at a disadvantage.

The problems that arise for the transsexual, particularly the post-operative transsexual stem mainly from the fact that, in Britain, until now, the birth certificate could not be changed. The birth certificate registers the sex of the child at birth and the fact that this may be altered by operative surgery later in life did not alter the basic situation in law. Thus legal circumstances such as marriage that require evidence of sex at birth reflected this inflexible situation.

A change of name by which you are known can, however, be altered without any necessity of legal processes. If one wishes to make more formal such a change however a statutory declaration may be made in front of a solicitor, or the name may be changed by deed poll.

Medical cards can be changed by sending a doctor's note to the local Family Health Services Authority. Income tax forms can be changed by going to the tax office with suitable proof of the new identity. A driving licence can be obtained by applying in the new name. Even the passport can be changed by writing to the local Passport Office with the appropriate confirmatory documents and letter from the medical adviser. A number of self help groups are available in Britain in addition to the Beaumont Society from whom advice can be sought if the transsexual becomes involved in a legal problem. The Albany Trust, the Transsexual Action Organisation and the Gender Trust are three of these. Equally, the National Council for Civil Liberties and Citizen's Rights groups are often helpful. The Campaign for Homosexual Equality, although primarily concerned with homosexual problems, will also offer guidance.

At the time of writing the law in Britain as it relates to sexual offences is in process of revision and it may well be that certain categories of offence, particularly those relating to homosexuality may be changed in a way which can also benefit the transvestite.

Shirley Maxwell writing in the Beaumont Bulletin, Volume 9, No. 3, comments on the Sex Discrimination Act. It is "an Act to render unlawful certain kinds of sex discrimination and discrimination on the grounds of marriage" and Shirley Maxwell reads the Act as prohibiting discrimination on the grounds of dress.

The relevant part of the Act is Part 1, Section 1b which states that a person discriminates against a woman if he applies to her a requirement or condition which he applies or would apply equally to a man but is such that the proportion of women who can comply with it is considerably smaller than the proportion of men who can comply with it and which he cannot show to be justifiable irrespective of the sex of the person to whom it is applied and which is to her detriment because she cannot comply with it.

Furthermore, in Section 2 (1) Section 1 relating to sex discrimination against men, the Act is to be read as applying equally to the treatment of men. Thus, Maxwell argues that if any authority attempts to tell a transvestite that they must not wear female attire in public then that authority is acting unlawfully unless it can show that it would equally not allow a woman to wear male attire. The wearing of clothes cannot be construed as likely to cause a breach of the peace unless materially similar behaviour on the part of a woman, such as wearing trousers could likewise be construed as likely to cause a breach of the peace. It would follow from this statement that any bye-law prohibiting men from dressing in female attire would be rendered illegal and should automatically be repealed as a result of the new Act.

At that rate any police officer making such an allegation would be liable to be accused by the victim of acting unlawfully, and could have an action brought against him which should stand up in court. The key to this argument lies in Section 5 (3) of the Act. It states *"a comparison of the cases of persons of different sex or marital status under the Section 1 (1) or 3 (1) must be such that the relevant circumstances in the one case are the same or not materially different in the other."*

This section would mean that if a man is charged with behaviour likely to cause a breach of the peace on the ground that he is dressed as a woman, then unless the person bringing the charge can show that he would equally charge a woman dressed as a man then the charge is unlawful by being discriminatory against a man on the ground of his sex. This point is yet to be tested to produce any case law.

The legal pitfalls for the transvestite vary considerably from one country to another, even between England and

Scotland. Some countries such as Holland and Denmark and many countries in South-East Asia exhibit total tolerance to the transvestite so that they can travel in public freely without fear. The situation in the United States of America varies state to state. Benjamin in his book *The Transsexual Phenomenon* states that criminality before the law is not necessarily criminality before science and common sense. Their interpretation of problems of behaviour such as homosexuality, transvestism and transsexualism as crimes creates criminals artificially merely by definition.

The New York State Code of Criminal Procedure Section 887 (7) may be used against transvestites. This law says that *"A person designated as a vagrant must not appear with a face painted, discoloured or covered or concealed or being otherwise disguised in a manner calculated to prevent him being identified."* This law is more than a century old and was passed for an entirely different purpose, being directed against farmers who disguised themselves as Indians and sometimes attacked law officers when they tried to enforce the unpopular Rent Law. Many transvestites, however, have been convicted and fined and indeed gaoled under this Act. Benjamin quotes a number of cases including one transvestite who dressed with the full knowledge of his wife who understood his problem and there was no testimony at the trial that he was engaged in any immoral criminal activity. The defence argued that Section 887 was unconstitutional as in violation of the due process of law provisions in the 14th. amendment of the constitution. The court ignored his testimony, however, and sentenced him to two days in the workhouse. The sentence was then suspended but when his employers learnt of the conviction, the man who was an airline pilot, lost his job and his eligibility for pension. The U.S. Supreme Court refused to review the case.

Another case quoted is that of a post-operative transsexual who was arrested for importuning. The plea that she was a woman was not believed and she was taken to the police station. There she was examined by a matron who told detectives that they had made a mistake. The charge was then changed to a charge of soliciting and she had to stand trial as a prostitute.

Benjamin states that arrests and convictions of transvestites for impersonation often with prison sentences regularly take place in the United States. When acquittal or probation takes the place of imprisonment it is not always due to clemency on the part of the court. It must be said, however, that Benjamin's book was written some years ago and that hopefully the present situation is somewhat more liberal than he implies. Sherwin, R.V., a lawyer writing in 1954 in the *American Journal of Psychotherapy* (Volume 8 part 9), in a short article on *"The legal problem in transvestism"* states that *"The question 'is it legal to be a transvestite?' is easier asked than answered."*

He goes on in the strict sense of the word there are no laws concerning either transvestism or the medical aspects of sex transformation but that the popular conception is that everything connected with the subject is illegal in the United States. Little or no objection is voiced except by those who become the unfortunate victims of such application.

There is no law which expressly forbids a man from wearing the clothes of a female but there are laws which forbid his doing so for the purposes of committing a fraud. Furthermore, in most States a wide and broad "disorderly conduct statute" is available for use by the authorities when all else fails. A male dressed as a female, in such a way that others might know merely by looking at him, might cause a crowd to gather and this can then come within the definition of disorderly conduct. No recent cases have however been brought.

With regard to the sex change operation there is no law which specifically prevents the performance of the operation subject to the consent of the patient. Some attorneys, however, have pointed to the Mayhem Statute which was a device to prevent men from becoming useless as fighters in the army. It was a serious crime in those days for a man to dismember in any way any limb or part of the body that would make him less able to fight. Yet this is still on the statute books and has been cited as a reason why such an operation would be a crime on the part of a doctor. In recent years, of course, operations have been performed but it is interesting to note that it is only some 25 years since such legal argument was being cited.

The situation in Australia is quoted in the Beaumont Bulletin Volume 9, No. 2. The criminal code of Western Australia has various offences under the general heading of "offences against morality", Sections 181 and 182 deal with unnatural offences, these being sodomy and bestiality. Under Section 184 it states that *"any male person who whether in public or private commits any act of gross indecency with another male person or procures him another male person to commit any act of gross indecency with him or attempts to procure the commission of any such act is guilty of a misdemeanour and is liable to imprisonment with hard labour for three years with or without whipping."*

This provision makes sexual behaviour by a transsexual unlawful whether in public or in private and whether or not they are consenting adults. Gross indecency has been defined as being unbecoming or offensive to common propriety. A decision of a Queensland court in 1955 *(Whitehouse Q.W.N. 76)* defines gross indecency as *"whether the tendency of the matter charged as obscene is to deprave or corrupt those whose minds are open to such immoral inferences."*

It has also been held *(R.V.Gammon, 1959, 49 Criminal Appeal Report 155)* that *"an intention on the part of the invitor to commit an immoral act accompanied by an invitation making it clear to the recipient what is intended will amount to an attempt to procure the commission of an act of gross indecency."*

The activities of the Chameleon Society, which is the equivalent of the Beaumont Society in Australia have been considered not to offend against this legal code. However, under Section 564 of the Criminal Code it is lawful for a police officer who believes on reasonable grounds that an offence has been committed to arrest that person without warrant, and the practical ramifications of this section could be that the transvestite in public might be subject to arrest if the police officer has grounds to suspect an offence has been committed.

The Chameleon Society specifically excludes transsexuals and it may be that had they been allowed as members that the legal advice would have been somewhat different.

The law is generally the same in other states in Australia, though in the state of Tasmania it was an offence for a male to appear in public dressed in women's clothes between the hours of 6.00 p.m. and 7.00 a.m! While the transvestite will in general only fall foul of the law in any of the countries which have been considered, if he goes out in public unwisely in such a way as to be easily spotted and risk cause for complaint, or if he makes some kind of exhibition which calls into question the possibility of soliciting, the transsexual can encounter a variety of difficulties which relate not so much to living publicly as a member of the other sex, but to questions relating to the legality of operative procedures, the changing of documents, and marriage or sexual relationships with those who on their birth certificate are of the same sex.

Since the phenomenon of the post-operative transsexual is relatively new, few countries have laws which were primarily designed to deal with such matters. So much variation exists within European law from total acceptance to total rejection, that it is not possible to review all the variations. We have looked at the situation as it applies in Great Britain and to some extent in the United States of America, the two countries where transvestite organisations are perhaps the most flourishing and organised and where because perhaps of the existence of the National Health Service in Britain, the operation has been enabled to be done for purely medical and ethical reasons and not for financial gain. An article by Julius Hoenig in the Canadian Medical Association Journal, Volume 116, part 9, 1977, outlines the legal position in a number of countries.

With regard to name change the procedures by which this can be done vary from country to country. In Canada, the United States and Britain it is legally acceptable simply to assume a new name as long as it is not done for a fraudulent purpose. It is usually advisable, however, to proceed with the formal legal requirements for a change of name through the court as this will subsequently make it easier to obtain changes on other documents. In many countries, however, a common-law change of name is not possible and a legal application with medical documents in support is required.

In most countries a change of birth certificate can only be made if it can be proved that a mistake was made at the time of the original issue. This applies in Canada and most of the United States. As Hoenig points out however, this is a very important point for the transsexual, yet it is nowhere clearly set out how the sex of the newborn is to be determined. It is usually left to the doctor or midwife to determine the sex. A panel of medical and legal experts set up by the New York Academy of Medicine following a court case *(Anonymous vs Weiner 59 Misc. Q.D. 380. 270 NYS) sup C Court Ct. 1966)* gave the following opinion: *"Male to female transsexuals are still chromosomally males. It is questionable whether laws and records such as birth certificates should be changed and thereby used as a means to help psychologically ill persons in their social adaptation."*

Recently the New Jersey Bureau of Vital Statistics made a decision to issue a birth certificate in a client's new name with the original sex designation crossed off and the new one added. *(Erickson, Educational Foundation Newsletter 9, no.1. 1976).* And in the United States 15 States now permit post-operative changes in the birth records. In two states in Canada (British Columbia and Alberta) a change in sex designation after gender confirmation surgery is possible on the birth certificate. The applicant is required to be unmarried and medical certificates need to be produced.

The Vital Statistics Act RSBC Ch.66, S21A states *"every birth certificate issued after the registration of birth is changed under this section shall be issued as if the original registration has been made showing the sex designation as changed under this section."* Marriage certificates are also included within the Alberta regulations.

In Switzerland since 1945 the Swiss courts have stipulated that gender identity is the proper criterion for determining sex in an operative transsexual and in 1969 a successful case was fought by Glaus. *(Schweiz, MED WOCHENSCHR 93 76/79 1963).*

The situation with regard to marriage of a post-operative transsexual is also controversial. In Britain the case of April Ashley *(Corbett versus Corbett)* achieved considerable fame and newspaper coverage. The question arose as to whether a marriage between a post-operative transsexual and a partner who was the same sex as that on the transsexual's original birth certificate, in this case therefore two men, was legally valid. The case arose out of the divorce action which had been instituted after the couple had been married for some time had to consider other complicated issues such as financial settlements, maintenance and so on.

Mr. Justice Ormerod in the High Court of Justice in England held that a marriage between a male-to-female transsexual and a man was void and that the contract should therefore be annulled. *(Corbett versus Corbett 2 ALL.E.R. 99 1970).* *"Marriage being essentially a relationship between man and woman the validity of the marriage depended on whether the respondent was or was not a woman and the respondent being a biological male from birth the so-called marriage was void."*

Justice Ormerod held that sex was determined by chromosomes, the gonads and the genitalia. Particularly if those three are concordant the sex of the patient is thereby determined. Gender identity as such, that is to say the subjective sense of gender is not held to be a criterion. The issue was raised further in the House of Commons in 1971 when the nullity of marriage bill came before the House. *(Hansard 814: 118: 1827ff)* The Corbett decision was upheld in this new legislation.

In 1976 the appellate division of the Superior Court of New Jersey unanimously declared that an individual who changes sex through surgery is entitled to all the legal rights enjoyed by others of the same sex including marriage and a marriage of a transsexual was valid as long as the transsexual told the partner in advance about the previous sex change operation. Thus the verdict of the English court was rejected and Judge Alan B. Handler set out in an 18-page document his reasoning. *(Erickson, Educational Foundation Newsletter 9 No. 1 1976).* Legislation in Sweden seems particularly pertinent to the problems of transsexuals and overcoming the difficulties which they have. Walinder *(Walinder, J and Thuwei: A law concerning sex reassignment of transsexuals in Sweden. Arch. Sex Behav. 5 255-258 1976)* states that the law came into force in 1972 and in the first two years some 60 individuals, approximately 50% male-to-female and 50% female-to-male transsexuals, had been dealt with under its provision. Under the law the responsibility for the decision to grant sex reassignment to an applicant rests with a national board which appoints a special committee possessing expert medical and legal knowledge to deal with these matters.

Three expert counsels, one representing psychiatry, one endocrinology and one jurisprudence are consulted which also deal with the question of sterilisation and castration. If the application is approved the national council instructs the parish office to change the entry in the parish register and to authorise other offices to make appropriate changes in the various documents with regard to the assignment of sex.

Certain conditions for sex reassignment are laid down under this Act. The applicant must have been found to present the syndrome of transsexualism and be incapable of reproduction.

He or she must be over 18 and a Swedish citizen and unmarried at the time of application. There has to be a trial period of at least a year after the initial change of name during which time the patient lives in the new gender role and is maintained under observation. Operations on the sex organs are not made a condition for granting authority for change of gender, although it is normally the practice. The new gender role becomes incontestable in court once it has been assigned and is irreversible.

This humane law would seem to remove the major problems which transsexuals encounter in many other countries, namely that their legal status can at all times and in all respects be questioned in court where countries do not have such a law. Similarly their social and legal status cannot be regularised in Britain by one action in court to settle the matter and many battles may consequently have to be fought over the years. The transsexual in Britain often finds that their social and legal status is that of one sex in some respects and still of the opposite sex in other respects which is clearly an unsatisfactory situation for all concerned.

It seems likely however that European law will cause many of these situations to have to be redressed and cases are coming before the European Court currently, contesting some of the applications of English law as it applies to gender consignment.

Transvestism and the Church
Revd. David Horton

Introduction

For centuries Western European culture has been moulded by the Christian faith. Many of those ideas have been exported around the world. Today Christian churches are found in every part of the world (sometimes illegally), from Antarctica to Lapland. Parts at least of the Bible have been translated into more than two thousand languages, and as a result it has been the world's best selling book for forty-nine of the last fifty years.

There is no such thing as the Christian Church as such. There are large international groups of churches such as the Roman Catholic, Orthodox and Anglican with many millions attending services every week around the world. There are also hundreds of smaller groups, many of whom pride themselves on their independence. Under the circumstances it is not surprising that there is no single view about transvestism (or many other issues). Individual ministers and church congregations will vary widely as to how they see the issues involved. Thus for example, the transgendered *fa'afafine'* in Samoa are found in many churches there as youth leaders, etc., because they know something of both sexes and have had a 'cultural niche' in church and society for over a century.

Why should there be a special problem? The central belief of the Christian faith is that God actively cares about all of us, and has made this world a place where challenges push us to grow in love and wisdom. God entered this planet's life as Jesus of Nazareth to show this love directly. Executed as a political activist, he burst through death, assuring us that we too can survive this life, and used this death as a way to take into himself, and enable him to forgive us, the hurts and damage we do to God, the world, ourselves and others. All we have to do is to ask for his help and it will be there – uncomfortable at times, admittedly. The Bible puts it this way: *'God is for us, so who can condemn. He who freely gave up his own life for us in Christ, will he not give us all we need.'* (from Romans chapter 8). Jesus taught his followers to call God 'Father' in a word that means 'Daddy'. Good news (= gospel) for everyone, including people who are transgendered. Of course God wants us to clear up a few problems in our lives along the way! We are all in messes of some kind at times. God wants to be there with us, helping. 'Whoever comes to me I will not turn away'. Which leads on to looking at why churches are often hostile.

Churches

First, please give people in the churches some credit! Most charities, hospitals, schools, and universities in this country were started by Christians, or based on their ideas. An amazing amount of individual good is still done by church members. Many Christians do care, and will try to help. Sometimes that means challenging what people are doing. Let's face it, if your neighbour's house is on fire then it doesn't say much for you if you don't at least warn them! Many church people see you as that neighbour! Some aren't very good at putting themselves in other people's shoes, which may mean they don't come across to you very well, perhaps because they are speaking out on the basis of unease they haven't really thought through. Even if some Christians can't understand what is involved, transgendered people should try to see other peoples' point of view – surely this is part of portraying 'her'?

Please also remember that Christians, like the rest of us, are subjected to lots of propaganda by the society around us. Television, newspapers, books, and videos often portray the transvestite and transsexual in ways that cause genuine worry. Things are much better now than twenty years ago or even than ten years ago when this guide was first published, but there is often still the feeling that it is sleazy and somehow wrong.

But let's face it, religion arouses strong feelings, and as a result can do immense harm as well as wonderful good. Someone will always be there to say: "God must be worshipped our way. If you do things differently you must be stupid, mad or bad! And when you don't change your ways when we say so that takes care of the first of those. So we are entitled to abuse you, lock you away from right thinking people, or kill you." All this done in the name of the God of love! And so we have the intolerance, the bigotry, the persecutions and inquisitions. All religions feel uncomfortable with dissent, look at what that twentieth century religion – Communism – has done to thousands of those under its power. Gender dissent is perhaps one of the most disturbing types.

The Christian churches have two thousand years of historical baggage to cope with, plus another slice borrowed from the early Jews. That can make for a great deal of rigidity. Equally it can get people away from the current hysterias. At the heart of that tradition is the Bible. So let's look at what it says on the subject. This won't take long, because it doesn't say much!

Deuteronomy 22 verse 5

This was part of the code of rules laid down in the Law of Moses to guide the Israelite nation. It says 'women mustn't dress in men's things', and adds that 'men shouldn't dress in women's clothes' either (the two words are different and the first might include using weapons or tools - tough on women soldiers or engineers). The word used to describe this behaviour is translated 'an abomination'. This word usually refers to some aspect of worshipping false gods - idolatry. There is good evidence that most ancient fertility religions went in for cross-dressed prostitution as part of their rituals, and that some of what happened was pretty unsavoury. So it is probably this that is being condemned. To confirm this interpretation, the people talking about this verse down the centuries link it to sexual immorality. It is perhaps relevant that the sixteenth century Jewish teaching work the *Shulkan Arukh* allowed Jews to cross-dress in the feast of Queen Esther ('Purim') because it was for joy and not for immorality. So if women in church wear trousers for joy then presumably it is fine, otherwise they should go back to their dresses! This verse was used to justify the burning at the stake of Joan of Arc (it had nothing to do with her making herself a major nuisance to both the English and French leadership, of course). I believe two minor women saints also lived as men, so it wasn't always fatal! Down the centuries a number of male clergy have lived as women as well, notably the Abbé de Choisy.

Genesis 1 verse 27

"Male and female he created them"

This is sometimes used to 'prove' that men and women are separate and that the boundaries shouldn't be blurred or crossed. This is an interpretation that doesn't sit too easily with the wider roles open to women today, and which also ignores natural sex changes in some lower animals and fish. My interpretation would be that this passage says that women are human too, and not second-class people!

1 Corinthians 6 verses 9-10

The 1611 King James 'Authorised Version' of the Bible includes in its list of those who will not have a place in the Kingdom of Heaven a group it translates as 'effeminate'. The word actually means 'soft'. When Jesus ironically asks people whether they went out into the desert to see John the Baptist because of his fine clothes the account uses this word for 'fine'. The particular meaning of this word in a sexual context is most probably 'seducer', although 'adulterer' is another possibility. Another word used in this passage means either a pederast or a homosexual, (which in Roman culture was often the same thing). Neither group is directly related to modern transgenderism in any way.

And that's it! Basically one verse in the sixty-six books which make up the core of the Bible, plus a couple that can be misunderstood as applying. There are other verses about clothes in Deuteronomy: about not blending materials in clothes (health risks?) and on adding fringes to cloaks (to separate Jews from the Canaanites?) which we ignore, as we do nearly all the rest of the laws which guided the Israelites. If you are gay, and a few cross dressers are, then there are various verses about that (and many publications that look at those verses and what they mean). If you are transsexual, the passage in Deuteronomy 23 verse 1 about eunuchs might apply, but if it does so too do the positive later verses in Isaiah 56 and Acts 8.

If to be transgendered is a gift, part of Gods built-in variation in the human race, surely God doesn't make mistakes and such people are meant to be this way (see Psalm 139). How they use their gift is what matters. If however, it is seen as a medical problem (as it often is, particularly by transsexuals), then God approves helping the person concerned to overcome the difficulties involved. This may be by changing over their social role, by coping while staying in their birth gender role or perhaps by 'visiting' the other gender role from time to time. Either way of looking at it means that it cannot be 'sinful' to be transvestite or transsexual, particularly when this need can first appear before the child is four, and is nearly always there by the early teens. It then comes down to what they do (and what others do to them) and why – in other words, ethics.

Ethics

Cross-dressing has an ethical dimension. Does it take up too much of the person's life? It has to be weighed against the rest of his life and responsibilities. If a family man spends money on 'her' clothes which has been set aside for a family holiday I would regard that as selfish and wrong. If he is married and spends more of their budget on 'her' activities than on his wife's at the very least it is not very tactful. If he can only help with the household chores while 'dressed' then perhaps he needs to think harder about his partner.

Again, if he says to others; "This is how I am. I can't change and so you will just have to live with it!" then it doesn't show much appreciation of other people's feelings. It often takes years for the transgendered person to come to terms with their difference. Surely it is unreasonable to expect someone else without this inner knowledge to cope or understand without a lot of gentle explanation and support? Most people have no problem with their 'gender identity'. It is thus very difficult for them to understand what is going on. As a result all sorts of wrong assumptions are likely to arise, and need to be worked through. Equally the cross-dresser may need to find out more. For many transgendered people their behaviour starts while they are young and they need to come to terms with themselves as adults.

Many of the ethical implications involved in being a cross dresser are not radically different to those involved with some hobbies: golf, playing a musical instrument, or taking part in amateur dramatics for example. They all take time, money, and effort! Sometimes they are more akin to the problems of addiction, when this area gets badly out of balance with the rest of life. Or perhaps they may have parallels to those of being disabled in a world of whole people.

There is one aspect that worries people sometimes, that of 'masquerade'. As I noted above, for someone with no inner conflict with his or her gender role in life there can be great difficulty in understanding what is happening. They see the efforts some transgendered people make to blend in with the other sex and assume it has to do with taking advantage of others. Thus if a transvestite visits a ladies' toilet (in the absence of a disabled one), for example, it must be to take advantage of women (there is a much simpler reason!) Down the centuries both Jewish and Christian commentators on Deuteronomy 22 verse 5 have assumed that cross-dressing was for immoral purposes. It is hard for others to appreciate that the transvestite is concerned to satisfy an inner need to see themselves in some sense as a woman, and to visit and enjoy time as their idyll. Problems here can be made worse where the transvestite is operating sufficiently in fantasy mode that he looks outrageous (and doesn't realise or doesn't care). The cross-dresser who can only portray his image of a woman on rare occasions may dress too young and revealingly. Sometimes he may compete with a wife or partner. Since men are visually stimulated, the adopted role may also have an erotic aspect that may be disturbing. They may 'fancy' not themselves, but the image they have created in the mirror. Many women's clothes have an erotic aspect for all men, of course.

There is no reason why 'she' shouldn't make a special effort from time to time, and there are plenty of clubs and venues around the country where dressing up for a special occasion is appropriate. But the man who chooses to go shopping or post a letter in 4" high heels, mini-skirt and satin blouse should not be surprised if what he is doing is misunderstood!

There is a simple rule that Jesus gave us: "Treat others as you want them to treat you."

Finding a welcoming church.

For some cross-dressers their woman's role is such an important part of who they are that they wish to express it before God in communal worship. When looking for a church they will need to recognise the difficulties that may arise.

As well as the Bible and the traditions of that particular group of churches, every congregation will have three things underlying its attitudes: how much it cares, what is the cultural background and understanding of its members, and some good old fashioned fear of the different or unknown. Which is why many Christians who cross-dress have to search to find a place where they will be loved and accepted. But such churches are there. How can they be found? Well broadly speaking, the more organised they are the less likely they are to welcome and accept. Some churches represent security in a rapidly changing world, and the transgendered person may represent an unwelcome example of that change. Many churches calling themselves 'Evangelical', 'Community' or 'Gospel' will not be accepting. Some will. On the other hand churches that welcome 'different' people: gays, immigrants, drug-addicts and the like are more likely to be open. I know a number of people who have been welcomed into Church of England and Methodist congregations, and others who have found the Metropolitan Community Churches to be accepting. Friends (Quaker) meetings have also been recommended. There is a group in the UK called 'Sibyls' (which means 'wise women') where some have found spiritual help as well.

But let's be brutally honest. Some people are their own worst enemies! If you go into a service with the attitude "This is me. Take me or leave me!" they will probably leave you, or rather ask you to leave them. If you dress presentably and are relaxed and open then there may well not be a problem. Remember that for many today, often the older people, it is a scary world out there, and someone keeps on selling the idea that it is the people who are different who do horrible things, who are the thieves and muggers and pedophiles. The minister who might want to be welcoming will have to look over his shoulder at the risk of scared mothers removing themselves and their children from temptation or danger. The congregation which has spent years making their church attractive may worry that numbers and income may fall if they start welcoming outsiders (the very people Jesus said he had come to help). Getting through life if you don't conform requires a good sense of humour, or at least of irony!

If you see a church that looks warm and friendly you can perhaps send 'him' to check it out.

If it looks promising then the best thing is to arrange a private interview with the minister. Your chances are much better if he is your ally, and if he's not then the sooner you know the better.

There are many transgendered people around the world contributing their skills and love to local churches. Many never need to make their difference open. Some by the quality of their life have persuaded neighbours and friends that they are genuine people of faith and love and opened the way to tolerance of others. For yet others hurts have required healing, sometimes on both sides. The Christian churches are there to bring together native and foreigner, rich and poor, young and old, male and female. Transgendered people are in there somewhere with their unique gifts and situations! I rejoice that a number have become my good friends.

One last personal point. The first five times I was reminded I wore a long dress in Church every Sunday were quite amusing, but after that it did tend to pall. This sort of joke is probably best left until after you have become friends with the minister!

Transgender and the Law
Stephen Whittle

Issues regarding the Committing of an Offence
Cross Dressing is not illegal in the UK, nor is it illegal to go out in public wearing clothes of the opposite gender. It is, however, an offence to behave in a manner likely to cause a breach of the peace, or in a manner which may be regarded as insulting. Much depends on what members of the public suspect about what a transvestite male is doing, or how they feel about what they know he is doing. There are, however, occasions where transvestites and transsexuals have fallen foul of the criminal law and, also, there are equally occasions when they may be victims of a crime.

Insulting a Female
This offence may be invoked where a transvestite, or a mtf pre-op transsexual woman, has to use the ladies toilet. This is a situation to avoid, wherever possible, if you are a transvestite man, using a unisex disabled toilet, if one is available, unless you feel very confident about your ability to pass well. However it would be a good defence if a pre-op transsexual woman could show that she was undergoing treatment and was participating in the 'real life test'. In an emergency, most cafés and restaurants will allow customers to use their toilets on request. These are often undifferentiated and usually quiet. Under no circumstances should a transvestite enter a male toilet while cross dressed since, quite apart from the risk of being beaten up, he may be prosecuted for the more serious offence of soliciting or importuning. A pre-op female to male transsexual may use the male toilets, but any man has the right to complain, though the offence would likely be a breach of

the peace. For all post op transsexuals, it is likely that this offence is not valid.

Another difficult area is ladies' changing rooms in shops, which can produce the same offence. Some stores such as Selfridges, Marks & Spencers and Debenhams will allow transvestites to use the ladies' changing rooms providing, of course, the transvestite looks the part and is respectably dressed. It would be polite to speak to the manager first. Otherwise, the male changing rooms should be used.

Breach of the Peace

This is a catch all common law offence, in which the definition of what constitutes a breach of the Queen's Peace is especially vague. It is defined as a normal state of society and any interruption of that peace and good order which ought to prevail in a civilised country is a breach of that peace. This is horribly vague and the law does not insist that the offender is causing a breach of the peace, only that he or she is judged likely to.

Should a complaint be made by a member of the public, it is likely that the prosecution would be successful, even if the witness was in no way upset or disturbed by their observation. The fact that anybody can make a complaint about anybody else means that transvestites or transsexual people need to exercise common sense, staying out of trouble and not drawing attention to themselves by wearing provocative clothing in public.

If arrested by the police, and charged on the grounds of behaviour, they should, through the solicitor, be asked to prove who was insulted. The police witness should be asked why anybody should be insulted at seeing someone dressed in clothes of the opposite gender.

Insulting Behaviour

Common law includes such offences as insulting behaviour or causing a disturbance, but behaviour as a transvestite or transsexual would have to be pretty outrageous to risk arrest or prosecution. Sections 5 & 7 of the Public Order Act 1936 reads:

> "It will be a summary offence for any person in a public place or any public meeting:
>
> (a) to use threatening, abusive or insulting words or behaviour, or (b) to distribute or display any writing, sign or visible representation which is threatening abusive or insulting with intent to provide a breach of the peace or whereby a breach of the peace is likely to be occasioned."

A complaint has to be made to a police officer and it is a difficult offence to disprove. It is a summary offence, so it will be dealt with by a magistrates court and is unlikely to result in a prison sentence.

Gender Recognition Act

According to *Hyde v. Hyde, 1866,* marriage is the voluntary union for life of one man and one woman. However the first attempt at a definition came about in the case of *Corbett v. Corbett, 1971.* A transsexual person, April Ashley, had undergone reassignment surgery to become a woman. The case held that the treatment she received did not, for the purposes of matrimonial law, result in a change of the sex assigned to her at birth.

Subsequently, section 11 of the Matrimonial Causes Act, 1973, provided that a marriage is void if the parties are not respectively male and female, based on chromosomes, gonads and external genitalia. As intersexed people demonstrate, the definition of a person's sex in such terms is not straightforward. It has also been suggested that there is a distinction between male or female, and 'man' and 'woman'. However, this argument was dismissed in *Franklin v. Franklin 1990*. Despite its lowly status in precedent, the decision in *Corbett v. Corbett* has been profoundly influential in all areas of British Law, including the case of *R v. Tan 1983* referred to below.

Throughout many representations to the European Courts, the British Government has reiterated its view that the birth certificate is simply an historical record of the facts as they were known at the time of birth and therefore not open to change. It was also clear that the situation that transsexual people face offends against several provisions of the European Convention on Human Rights, and once the British Government signed up to it, it committed itself to making changes in British Law, which are, at the time of writing, awaiting the Royal Assent. Assuming that this is granted, the Bill will become the Gender Recognition Act (2004).

While marriage has been the issue that has been highlighted in publicity about the Bill, much more important to transsexual people is the control of the privacy of their personal and medical histories. The birth certificate that will be issued is not a change, but a replacement referred back to the original record, access to which will be strictly limited. The Gender Recognition Bill also bypasses the necessity to define sex, let alone gender, and leaves the way open for the medical panel to take note of advances in scientific knowledge.

There are, of course, many details to be sorted out, and other issues to be addressed. It is assumed that those people reading this book are not expecting to change their civil identity on a permanent basis. Those who are, are advised to consult more specialised literature.

Soliciting

This is governed by S.32 of the Sexual Offences Act 1956 where it is illegal for a man to persistently solicit or importune in a public place for immoral purposes. The police must be able to show whom the transvestite (or transsexual) was supposed to be soliciting, which implies that a one-off incident would not be relevant. In the case of a transvestite, evidence of heterosexuality, such as being married or having a girlfriend, will be a good defence.

The clear rule here is again to use common sense and never use the male toilets, avoid seedy bars, never stand around in public places, especially if provocatively dressed. A fetishistic or masochistic transvestite, as opposed to a gender motivated transvestite or transsexual, is particularly at risk of prosecution for soliciting or breach of the peace.

Since the case of *R v Tan (1983)* it was held that notwithstanding gender reassignment surgery, a person born male remains a man for the purposes of the Sexual Offences Act. Prior to the Gender Recognition Act, a post genital surgery mtf transsexual woman would still be charged with importuning in the same way that a transvestite would, carrying a greater sentence than if a genetic female was charged with soliciting. Also, a post op mtf transsexual woman could be charged with living off her own immoral earnings as was the case in *R v Tan (1983)*. The charges arose out of acts of prostitution performed by a woman, Moira Tan, and a mtf transsexual woman, Gloria Greaves, the proceeds being shared with a man, Brian Greaves. Gloria Greaves was convicted of being a man living on the earnings of Tan's prostitution, contrary to section 30 of the Sexual Offences Act 1956; and Brian Greaves was convicted of living on the earnings of prostitution by Gloria Greaves, contrary to section 5 of the Sexual Offences Act 1967.

However, it is intended that those who have gained legal recognition in their acquired gender under the Gender Recognition Act will be of their new sex for all legal purposes except historical events – such as fathering a child before gender reassignment. This will in effect overrule the principle in *R v Tan*.

Gross Indecency
The laws on homosexuality do not apply to transvestites or transsexuals but the fact remains that it is sometimes associated in the public mind as a form of perversion or homosexuality. Transvestites must be careful to assess whether anything that they do in company with another person could lead to misunderstanding. They may be suspected of engaging in homosexual activities even if soliciting or importuning is not in question.

Gross indecency, which is male homosexual lovemaking, ceased to be illegal under the Sexual Offences Act 1967, if certain conditions are met. These are that the act is in private and is with consenting males over the age of 16. If these conditions are not met then section 13 of the Sexual Offences Act 1956 applies, with a penalty of up to five years imprisonment. If more than two people are present then it is also possible to commit the offence of attempting to procure the commission of an act of gross indecency. Once again, common sense will avoid any potential problem with this offence.

Criminal Records Bureau.
Those seeking employment should be aware that a check with the Criminal Records Bureau is required, not only for working with children and vulnerable people, but also for people working with the public, such as taxi drivers, and

entering people's homes, such as repair people and fitters. Although the birth certificate is not officially proof of identity, the process normally starts with it. For post-op transsexuals, it means revealing their original status, and the CRB has a procedure in place to protect confidentiality. For transvestites, of course, this should not be a problem, nor for transsexuals, if the gender recognition process becomes a reality.

Prison

A transvestite and a pre-op mtf transsexual woman will almost certainly be sent to a male prison. However prison health services are now part of the National Health Service, so prisoners are now entitled to the same standard of health care. As such if a prisoner was receiving prescribed hormone therapy prior to imprisonment their hormone therapy should continue, unless some other health matter intervenes to make the continuance a threat to well being.

If a pre-op transsexual woman is facing incarceration then it is imperative that they disclose their status to the probation officer who is preparing their pre-sentence report. They can ask that the judge or magistrate does not disclose the information in open court, but this cannot be guaranteed. Generally a sympathetic approach will be taken, and the disclosure may actually result in an alternative (and better for you) sentence, which may not be custodial.

Post-operatively, under Gender Recognition Act, it will not be revealed in court, under pain of legal sanction, unless it has a bearing on the case. In the case of a pre-op ftm transsexual he will be sent to a female prison. At present, post op ftm's can be sent to either, which is very dependent upon the surgery which has been undergone. If phalloplasty has taken place then he may well be sent to a male prison. However, it must be said that many prison staff now have some experience of working with transsexual people, so they are open to the issues, but it must be remembered that prison is prison, and rarely an enjoyable experience.

Offences against the Person
The Transgender Person as Victim.

By and large, transvestites and transsexual people are sensible and use common sense to avoid trouble and contact with the law, but they face the same risks as any other person and there are occasions in which they may be victims of a crime. This is one area of the law where ftm transsexual men are likely to be more fortunate in not encountering the same degree of reverse gender discrimination and harassment.

Common Assault

They can be the victims of assault motivated by discrimination against them as a minority. Section 47 of the Offences Against the Person Act, 1861 applies, as it does to anyone else and it is an arrestable offence. The problem of reporting such an offence to the police is the risk of an unsympathetic view, and the fear that details of one's life history may come out in the courts. The possible newspaper publicity is enough to deter a transvestite, in particular, from informing the police. However, in recent years, police forces around the country have committed themselves to stopping hate crime of all sorts. Even if you don't wish to take it any further, most forces want to hear about it. As London's Westminster Police put it "we can't deal with crimes we don't know about" They give the Beaumont Trust's number as a confidential contact point.

This is of course an insidious position, but unless someone is prepared to push the case through the courts, I can only recommend, once again, that common sense is used, avoiding high risk public places, especially after pub closing times, with the risk of attracting unwanted attention from lager louts. There are the risks that every woman faces, in being assaulted or harassed, which means one should think and act as women do, not taking risks, such as being out alone after dark. I deplore the fact that this situation exists in society; a woman's freedom to do as she pleases is at risk and smacks of second class citizenship. The fact remains that there are members of society who will try to take advantage of women, with the consequence that we must all be aware of the risks. If you do decide to press charges, the Trust can supply information about the procedures and what to expect.

Sexual Assault.
The new Sexual Offences Act 2003 revises the law in this area specifically to support the victim. It should also be remembered that section 1 of the Sexual Offences (Amendment) Act 1992 makes it an offence to publish reports identifying the victims of indecent assault and other serious sexual offences unless they give their consent to being identified. In particular, with the exception of rape which must involve penile penetration, all sexual offences now apply equally to males and females of any sexual orientation. For the first time there is a definition of consent, where the person consents has both the choice, and has the freedom and capacity to make that choice. In addition, there are several new categories of offence.

Rape is now classified as penetration by the penis of somebody's vagina, anus or mouth, without their consent. Although not precedent, in 1996 a court in Reading found that the neo-vagina of a post-operative transsexual woman could be raped.

There is also a new offence of ***Assault by Penetration,*** whereby it is an offence to penetrate the anus or vagina of someone else with any part of the body or with an object, if the penetration is sexual and if the person does not consent.

Sexual Assault covers any kind of intentional sexual touching of somebody else without their consent, including touching any part of their body, clothed or unclothed, either with one's body or with an object.

Causing a person to engage in a sexual activity without consent, covers any kind of sexual activity without consent. For instance it would apply to a woman who forces a man to penetrate her, or an abuser who makes their victim engage in masturbation.

An important new law, with the prevalence of 'date rape' drugs is that of ***Administering a Substance with Intent,*** that is, to give someone any substance – for instance spiking their drink – without their consent, and with the intention of stupefying them so that sexual activity can take place. In this instance, sexual activity could include stripping someone or taking pornographic photos of them, even if the intended sexual activity did not take place, for instance when someone sees what is going on and intervenes to stop it. There are other offences where the penalty is more severe if there is the intention of committing a sexual offence.

The preceding section on the Sexual Offences Act 2003 is extracted from the Home Office Leaflet SOA/2 "Adults: Safer from Sexual Crime", available by post or from the website *http://homeoffice.gov.uk/sexualoffences/legisation/*

It, and the extract from the Public Order Act 1936, is reproduced under the terms of Crown Copyright Policy Guidance issued by HMSO

Counselling and Support

Personally Speaking
Diana Aitchison

When I found a pair of women's knickers (there was no other word for this drab, unfeminine garment) in my new love's sock drawer I was at first puzzled as to why they should be there. I could not imagine any mistress (past tense) ever wearing them so where did they come from? Why were they there?

This happened in 1984 and the word transvestite was one I was barely acquainted with, let alone having become acquainted with someone who was one. Yet within minutes the light slowly dawned – Jim wore these. I don't know how I knew, I just did. Several curious facts about him were beginning to fall into place, particularly the fact that he was the only man I ever knew who actually actively encouraged me to go shopping for myself, let alone insisting on accompanying me. There was his open admiration of all things feminine and female, for instance, which I found distinctly intriguing in a man who encompassed all things macho and male in his own world as a petrochemical engineer; Scottish to boot. Yet I still found it impossible to believe that Jim could possibly want to wear women's clothes. Anyway, it was only a pair of knickers wasn't it?

I have never been able to remember how long the passage of time was between discovery and confrontation – probably only a few days although it seemed like forever. We were living in Kuwait at the time and I was totally on my own when it came to having someone to talk to about it. I had made several friends among the other wives there but I instinctively knew that this was something that was not going to be aired for discussion in our small community. A man's reputation was everything to him in the hostile desert arena of oilrigs and I was not going to betray Jim, however angry I was becoming. I didn't even really know why I was angry except that this was a secret that I hadn't been let in on and I wasn't very sure that I wanted to know about it anyway. By now my fevered imagination was littered with visions of seedy gay clubs where everyone looked like Danny la Rue and I was beginning to feel more than a little stupid too. How could I fall for a man like this, let alone follow him thousands of miles to an unknown territory where I was isolated from everyone and everything that was safe and familiar to me? I had divorced my first husband, the father of my two children, by then young adults, many years before and I didn't want to make another disastrous choice. I had to know what meaning these knickers had for Jim.

I held up the knickers and asked "What are these?"

"Oh," he said, at once both alarmed and embarrassed. "I thought I had got rid of all of them."

"All of them?"

"Well, it is just a fetish thing – you know – after all I have lived the single life for so long since separating from my wife, and I have never been a womaniser. Anyway, I don't need them now – I've got you haven't I?"

He went on to promise that it wouldn't go any further, but of course it did.

Over the ensuing years we have battled and fought, compromised and come to a level of understanding about each others needs that stretches far beyond the 'live happily ever after' ideals of our original courtship. Little by little, Jim started to trust me enough to relate to me the disgust and guilt that he felt about having the need to put on 'women's' clothes from time to time. He explained how these feelings started in childhood and how they contradicted the strong religious upbringing that had been the mainstay of his

Presbyterian parents' background. By the time he was old enough to understand about sexuality he became aware that he was not 'gay' which seemed to be another contradiction, given the little knowledge he had gained in the playground about men who wore female clothes. His first marriage, that survived a long and gruelling twenty eight years, was to some extent an institution entered into in direct opposition to his innermost feelings.

Although he genuinely loved his wife and children, the marriage was overshadowed by the torment of his gender confusion, made worse by the emergence of the first 'sex-change' operations. His feelings alternated between sheer hatred of his male identity and envy towards these 'new women', to actually protecting and often over-promoting his male side – classic behaviour in men who are gender dysphoric, the blanket term for any form of cross gender confusion in either sex. He told me many years ago that if he thought that he could make a better woman of himself than he was as a man then he might have thought further about pursuing gender reassignment surgery. However, he knew in his heart of hearts that he could never be successful as a transsexual woman and besides this he actually preferred having the choice of being 'male' or 'female' as the mood dictated, thus accepting that he was a transvestite.

For myself, as his wife, there have been sacrifices that, if I had been asked all those years ago, if I was willing to make, then no doubt I would have said "No way." Our's is not a conventional marriage, but I am not a 'door-mat' wife either. I had no idea what the future held for me when, a year after discovery, I agreed to marry Jim. At that time, everything seemed to be under control; the crossdressing was an occasional pastime only. Jim said he needed it to relax, to get down from the male 'pedestal' from time to time. I was having a problem with my own femininity that seemed to be under assault every way I turned. I didn't want to be constantly told that I was so 'lucky' to be born a woman and somehow be made to feel guilty about a simple fact of life, and I didn't want to exchange roles in order to 'compliment' his female persona. I tried to kid myself that the crossdressing was just a passing phase that, under the right circumstances, would go away, even though it had dominated Jim's life up until then.

There have been many times when I have felt that it would be better for us to part; then I have reminded myself that Jim has never chosen to be a crossdresser, the preferred term for a heterosexual transvestite. I know now that he couldn't tell me the truth about his feelings when he first met me because he didn't have an explanation himself. He knows that he isn't always easy to live with - his mood swings can be appalling although they have reduced considerably over the years. He now has a hard-won freedom to dress when he likes, within reason, based on rules about budgeting and curbing the more obsessive elements that are the hallmarks of what some people see as a bizarre form of gender expression. However, being aware of the pleasure and contentment that he receives from his cross-gendered times, who am I to deny him those moments?

Spending much of his life being suppressed by a hostile and somewhat unforgiving society has left Jim with a cynical view of reality which he tries to offset by being caring and giving to the people he loves; the traits which drew me to him in the first place. I married him knowing that he would try his hardest to be the husband, the man, that I then expected him to be, and I made a pact with myself that I would try my hardest for him to be the wife he wanted me to be. As we are ultimately just mere mortals we have occasionally failed; myself in having to admit that I cannot cope with crossdressing in the bedroom and Jim having to realise that there are some demands that he cannot make on me via his more outlandish fantasies. We have tested each others' courage and steadfastness to the limit, to the extent of 'coming out' in public in 1990 which was both nerve wracking and a great source of relief to us both. We had become so paranoid about being 'found out' that, in the end, exposure at the request of Robert Kilroy in an article about modern marriages probably saved our sanity. It was the ultimate therapy, enabling us as it did to admit to the world that we wanted to live in openness and honesty, at peace with ourselves. Our first families know our story and are supportive in as much as they respect our right to live our life in the way we do. Jim chooses not to dress in front of them, and the younger grandchildren have not been told, although the teenagers are aware that grandpa has a need to crossdress. It has been a difficult journey for Jim's own sons, not surprisingly, given that the image they have of their father is one of a typical hot-headed Scottish engineer, as strong and uncompromising as the fathers of their contemporaries on a tough Glaswegian housing estate. They are adults now with their own families and we make no apologies for not shielding them from the facts about their father. Indeed, hopefully, it has helped them come to a deeper understanding of the needs that have driven their father all his life to try to be the person that everyone, his parents in particular (as he is an only child) wanted him to be. That it has saddened them, embarrassed them and at times made them angry is regrettable; no one wants their children to suffer the disillusionment that the children of crossdressing fathers may have to face.

At the same time though, perhaps they are able to come to terms with fact that their father may be the bravest man they will ever know. Jim has risked alienation and ridicule from his family members and past acquaintances in order that the truth about this distressing gender-contradiction that affects a surprisingly large number of men can be learned about and understood at some time in the not-too-distant future.

I had yet to learn about Gender Dysphoria, which I now know is not just a 'behavioural problem' but something that is within Jim that cannot be denied. His need to express a female side is stronger than both of us. The first books I read on transvestism seemed to suggest that dysfunctional parenting caused it; the same was applied as the cause for homosexuality. What puzzled me was the fact that if this was caused by 'nurture' why couldn't it be corrected by the psychiatrist's magic wand? I used to suspect that it wasn't a learned behaviour like gambling, where the adrenaline-rush carries the gambler on a pleasurable, if often disastrous journey, but can be 'cured' by the appropriate therapies. I learned that many transvestites had been subjected to what appeared to me to be appalling treatments at the hands of an earlier school of behavioural scientists. Everything from aversion therapy to electric shock treatments to try to make these men stop what seemed to be unnatural and perverted habits were attempted but nothing worked. Despite their best efforts, the psychiatrists of the day were losing the battle. That left 'nature' as the only alternative explanation and, as we start the new century, scientists are becoming more knowledgeable about the part of the brain that determines our sense of gender and gender identity.

Despite the difficulties that Jim's gender dysphoria has brought to our relationship, I am heartened by the discovery that my husband is not a deliberately awkward, and sometimes infuriating, person to live with - it's just the way he is made. He would probably have some of his traits and habits even if he weren't gender dysphoric - we are all products of our socialisation as well as our genetic or chromosomal make-up. Much as I longed at one time to believe if it weren't for the crossdressing "everything would be perfect"; realistically, I have come to understand that the cross dressing was just an excuse for me to make whenever life was less fulfilling than the expectations I had endowed it with. Now I can stand back and view him objectively if he is being particularly obsessional or moody and remind myself that these moments will pass and he will be calm and kind once again.

Jim has rewarded my efforts to try to understand him by supporting me through University when I eventually attended as a mature psychology student. Despite our trials and tribulations I believe that we have both grown emotionally and spiritually even though Jim is less likely to admit this about himself. He will always have a part of him that is private to him. I feel secure enough to not want to invade that private space and at the same time he has come to learn that he cannot have 'all' of me. I am my own person too now, and can accept his alter ego Jenny as someone who shares his life and eases the stressful times that sometimes threaten to overcome him. In a sense 'she' is his personal therapist and she has learned that though I am pleased to see her I do not have to make fundamental changes to myself to accommodate her.

A Cure for Transvestism
Jed Bland

The aim of this book was, and still is, to review the subject for the benefit, not only of transvestites themselves, but the professionals they might approach. Not least to ameliorate the pathologising approach of most textbooks. The idea of a cure would be uppermost in many reader's minds. Why else would they visit a doctor? It was also a background theme to many calls to the helpline, especially from those who felt under pressure from their wives and families.

A few years ago, I was present at a seminar, given at a London hospital where a counsellor described a family whose four year old son, the younger of two boys, seemed to be too fond of play that involved dressing in his mother's clothes. What I liked particularly about this story was that the whole family loved the boy enough to attend as a family and, moreover, review their own behaviour. Family therapy resulted in the boy being able to make a group of friends at school, instead of being teased, with the likelihood of becoming a solitary. Further, the counsellor set out to preserve the boy's great sensitivity and imaginative powers, by encouraging him to dress up as a wizard, for instance.

At the end, a transsexual who was also present said to me, "I wonder if he really will stop cross-dressing?" and I said, "I hope not!", meaning that I hoped that he wouldn't do so if he still needed to. I felt, rather than heard, a gasp from behind us, and realised that many of the others in the audience were obsessed with the cross-dressing as the problem. They were unable, or unwilling, to look past the behaviour to the child himself.

It illustrates my feelings about traditional health practice and social work in which power is gained by 'treating' or 'helping' the 'patient' or 'client' and counselling which is concerned with the person him or herself. The first thing a counsellor (or a helpliner) has to learn is humility.

In their search for a 'cure' for transsexualism (and also for being gay), or to legitimise it, scientists have highlighted certain physiological and genetic factors, which feminise boys and masculinise girls. Let us suggest that all that this shows is that there is a natural variation in both boys and girls; nobody has yet shown how a boy can become homosexual, transsexual, or simply a gentle man.

The motivation to find biological causes, which would excuse the way we are, and to find the technology to make us the way we think we ought to be, denies us the freedom to be ourselves, to grow and to win (or to fail) by our own endeavours. In fact, science is increasingly demonstrating what we always knew – that each of us is a unique individual. Let us all be who we individually are, rather than who we 'should' be.

There is no doubt, of course, that men are different from women. It is also true that the difference between boys and girls is much smaller. The physical natural differences are magnified and reinforced by cultural expectations, perhaps in ways that oppress, rather than guide infants at the edges of the natural variation in people.

Development through life is a long process of experiencing, learning and teaching, first studied by Freud, with his description of the conflict between the libido, the ego and the super-ego. The significance of the super-ego is that it may contain pressures from outside that cannot be incorporated in to the ego. Later, behaviourists suggested that we learn responses to various stimuli, like Pavlov's dogs, and once programmed, we cannot easily change them. The existence of any sort of free will is therefore denied. In everything we do, we negotiate a path through a complicated network of reinforcements. Though behaviourism gave an elegant, and still valid, model for learning, it was only a model, and incomplete.

The so-called Social Learning approach theory suggested that what we do is learnt, to an extent by imitating others. Some imitation is reinforced. Some is discouraged. Moreover, having been learnt, they can be unlearnt. Then came the Cognitive approach that many of our behaviours are intrinsic to our human nature. This tension between nature and nurture is ongoing and unlikely to be resolved soon in such a highly politicised area as gender.

To my mind, the common feature of all these theories is that they deal with the way behaviours are adopted by the person, from the outside, as a passive recipient.

Attention is beginning to be given (even in education) to the mental processes of the person, as an active organism which is not just a passive target for imposed learning, but having an innate motivation to explore.

Remembered experiences are organised according to their relevance to each other, and the reaction to them, thus mind could be described as the way an individual brain organises memory. Accordingly, structures of memorised data are built up through life, sometimes called schemas or constructs. Usually such schemas go so far back into childhood, that we cannot remember their beginning. Some memories may be too painful to recall. Integral to these schemas is the way that, at the time, we interpreted, sometimes conflicting, experiences.

It follows then, that no two people have exactly the motivations for cross-dressing, and the central dictum of counselling is that the client is the expert in his, or her, own life.

The telephone helpline.
Often the call to a phoneline is the first important step, the moment when the TV admits for the first time to himself what he is, the end of denial. Many calls are silent ones, the caller gets through, then cannot bring himself to speak.

Often there may be several calls, spread over many months, sometimes lasting an hour or more. Sometimes, someone will phone very nervously and, after a little general talk, there will be a long silence, then he will say "I can't do it. Do you mind if I ring off?" Usually they don't ask, which can become very discouraging for the operator, who must remember that he, or she, has been 'there' for them. One day such callers may be able to confront their feelings and put them into words.

Many people simply telephone for a chat. The message is, often, of relief that there is someone to talk to; they couldn't possibly reveal their address to receive mail, nor could they consider joining a group or appearing at a meeting. Usually, there is no way of sending literature and, now that calls can be traced back, many callers are asking if they are being traced or taped. Some ask for advice or tacit permissions that cannot be given, and are resentful that they haven't been given the solution to their problems. In particular the permission to confess to a wife is fraught with danger, since there is no way of predicting her reaction.

While some callers wish to talk of sexual matters, the phoneline does not provide contacts. It is made clear that any phone numbers that may be offered are for social groups. However, phonelines respect feelings, whatever they are, and acknowledge their validity. They offer the opportunity to put thoughts into words, to make them concrete, and put them into order. Many callers are very frightened and highly emotional; they call for great gentleness. Sometimes the issues may be as serious as a mother mutilating herself, or a husband who has to "bribe" his wife to give him sexual satisfaction, because he cannot bear to feel love. Or another who drinks to avoid cross-dressing, then drinks to have the courage to do so, the frustration causing him to physically assault his wife and family. In situations like this, the telephone cannot provide any real level of counselling. Sometimes, after callers finish, operators often wish they had a magic wand. They may have to work on their own feelings, to terminate the call for themselves, after the phone has been put down.

Counselling.
The social groups offer friendship and facilities. They do not, or should not, offer advice that should come from a professional counsellor. 'Coming Out' is not a 'once and for all' overnight process. For many people, it involves a long period of soul-searching and self-analysis. Counselling provides the conditions to find answers.

Counsellors, increasingly, are being invited to work with general practitioners. Others are employed by such groups as RELATE and MIND. There are many in private practice, who should be listed as 'registered counsellors' by a recognised organisation, such as The British Association for Counselling, or the United Kingdom Register of Counsellors. The Beaumont Trust can offer the names of counsellors who have a special interest in gender problems. Charges are reasonable, around £30-60 an hour, scaled down accordingly to ability to pay, and it is usual to contract for about six sessions initially.

Such counsellors, themselves, have to confront their own social learning, at a very fundamental level, whether as a gay or a 'straight' person. Put another way, they have to put their very identities to one side. This may be why people say, "I prefer to talk to another TV, because he will understand." Each and every one of us views the subject through our own individual cultural and personal distorting lens. It is a problem that bedevils feminist and gay critiques, even sober scientific studies. As Bem puts it in *The Lenses of Gender:* "A fish is unaware that its environment is wet. After all, what else could it be?"

The experience of counselling is likely to feel strange to the person who has not tried it before. Unlike the conventional idea of going to see an 'expert' who will tell the person what to do, and perhaps give him, or her, treatment, it is a relationship, sometimes a very deep one.

The basis of counselling is that the client is coming to the counsellor for help. Therefore, he is disempowered; the counsellor has the power in the relationship. The aim is for the client to take back the power over his life. So there is a relationship of equality where the client and counsellor work together to find solutions and make plans.

In general counselling, the issue may be something like overcoming feelings of loss at, on the one hand, losing one's job or, on the other, losing a loved one. Various counsellors help with neuroses, allergies, loneliness, shyness, coming to terms with sexuality, family strife, physical, emotional and sexual abuse, substance abuse, depression, indeed every kind of life experience that one might have difficulty in coping with.

Counselling is often seen as the giving, or rather the offering, of advice and of the negotiation of practical problems. What is much more important to the counsellor, however, is the feelings of the person disempowered by the practical issue. Because transvestism is very much to do with feelings, these are the focus of the relationship. The emphasis is not what is bad about the clients, but what are the good things they are doing for themselves and how they are preventing themselves from doing the good things they want to do.

By listening to the client recounting his, or her, story, the counsellor divines the questions he, or she, is asking. By reflecting the questions back, the hope is that the client can find answers. This is the answer when people say "I don't want counselling. They wouldn't understand." The answer is "Then tell them. Let them understand."

It has to be said that the result of counselling may be unexpected. The TV may want to stop cross-dressing at the start, but by the end, decide to enjoy it in innocence and set out to develop both roles. He may previously have had negative feelings about himself as a person and may go on to find new assertiveness, with social and relational skills. In fact, the aim of counselling is not "to make the person stop dressing," but to give him the power to choose when and where and how he will dress.

Relationships.

Like most people, the transvestite may have married someone from a similar background, or with a similar viewpoint on life. Small wonder that the divorce rate is so high among transvestites and that they are often reluctant to try again, though the cross-dressing is rarely, in itself, the sole cause for the breakdown of the relationship.

Usually, it is one or the other partner that approaches a helping organisation and, often, it is a transvestite's wife that makes the first move. Counselling one partner in isolation is usually unavoidable, at first. There is an ethical dilemma in dealing with only one partner in a relationship, either by phone or face to face, but this belongs totally to the client. However, even if the counselling process remains unknown to the other partner, the changes it brings about will be reflected in the dynamics of the relationship, often disruptively.

It is not invariably a good thing for a transvestite to confess to his partner, yet one cannot always go on for ever in secrecy, and discovery is likely to be disastrous.

It follows then that counselling can talk about ways of confessing in a way that a telephone conversation can't. The issues involved can be explored in depth. The transvestite can first resolve his own confusion and work out what his partner's feelings are likely to be. The aim may be to work towards inviting the partner into the counselling relationship. Often this may be more acceptable to the partner if the counsellor is clearly outside the transvestite community, a worker with RELATE, for instance.

Once couple counselling begins, the counsellor is likely to sit back and work with the dynamics of the relationship, in the hope that it can be redefined in a way that helps both partners. It may seem odd to suggest this, but the fact is, that the couple's relationship has already been irretrievably redefined by the fact of discovery or confession.

It is because transvestism (or transsexualism) is such an individual experience that person-centred counselling is so vital. An early aim might be to find out what good reasons there are for continuing both the marital and the counselling relationship. Even if there are good reasons, a satisfactory resolution will not, however, appear overnight.

The transvestite's wife finds herself having to re-evaluate her own preconceptions about gender roles. Does her husband really have to wear the trousers (in the metaphorical sense)? With the idea that her husband is not the man she thought he was, there may be the feeling that the very foundations of the marriage are shifting. If the truth comes out by discovery, she is likely to feel betrayed by all the years of secrecy and deceit. Even if it comes about by confession, she is suddenly given a problem that her husband has been working on for years, and he is probably no nearer to solving it than when he started.

Often it is seen as a pathology of the husband, who may feel very disempowered in the counselling relationship. Depending on his wife's feelings on entering counselling, she may also be feeling very confused and frightened. There are likely to be very strong emotional under-currents. Both the husband and wife will be hoping to find solutions and, being human, will have their own hopes. There are no quick answers and it will be all too easy for bridges to be burnt and unrealistic promises to be made.

In the first interview, there may be much talk about ways of 'not doing it.' One alternative is workaholism, which has obvious problems in terms of stress, and causing the TV to be less 'present' for his family. Another is tactical hiding of the clothes. In other words, instead of burning everything, which TV's do frequently, they hide them away, but make them difficult to get at. The idea is, that the TV knows they are available, in case he needs them, but when the urge occurs, he can decide it's too much trouble to get them out.

The TV's wife usually wants to know why her husband needs to dress up in women's clothes. It is as well to avoid being drawn into a long psychological discussion, which has little relevance to everyday situations. It could be suggested that, at some time in the past, he has been 'told' that certain feelings are 'unmanly'.

If there is a second meeting, the TV and his wife may have agreed to accept his transvestism into their lifestyle, conditionally, but still do not feel that they are "like those others." They may have seen a programme on television or seen a magazine article, which is a complete 'turn-off.' They may say they simply can't relate to the people they have seen. Generally, however, the talk revolves around present issues. It is made clear that the TV's wife has as much right to decide what happens as the husband, and that there must be a continuing dialogue based on sharing feelings - with mutual support, not resentful tolerance.

The counsellor should offer the warning that the husband, in being able to experience this new world of the mind, might go right 'over the top' for a while. Usually, at the start, the TV is like a little boy with a new toy, exploring all the new feelings that he has given himself permission to have. The hope is that he will work through them before his wife finally loses her patience. He must not forget his wife's wishes and needs. From time to time, he might, perhaps, put on his best suit and take his wife out to dinner. The aim is to shift the focus onto the couple and their lives together, away from the cross-dressing.

Having worked through these feelings, the TV settles down, with a new outlook on life. He feels able to slip into something comfortable to relax, or he may enjoy dressing up for an occasion, like the weekends around the country, where TVs, with their wives, may take over a complete hotel. The staff enjoy these meetings as much as the guests do, while the latter take the attitude that, if Society will accept their eccentricity, they will try not to give offence, and will try to behave responsibly.

Meanwhile, freed of the day-long obsession, the TV may approach his working and family life with new vitality, tempering his more chauvinistic attitudes within the family, while not becoming less 'manly.' His wife, too, may find the opportunity to express new attributes that she finds within herself. Those TVs who had negative feelings about themselves may go on to find an opportunity for real personal growth, and so may their wives.

Psychotherapy.

To quote Blanchard and Steiner: "uncovering or psychoanalytically orientated intensive therapy . . . . has not been shown to be useful." To some extent this may be due to misconceptions about psychotherapy. Just as many transexuals are said to see the consultant as an impediment to their progress towards reassignment, so transvestites may see the psychoanalyst as someone whose only aim is to stop them cross-dressing.

There is a considerable grey area between counselling and psychotherapy, with professionals in both disciplines disputing their territory. My definition is that counselling is 'present centred', while psychodynamics is 'past centred', and therapy is change, hopefully for the better. Part of the process may, unexpectedly, involve deciding what will be 'better' and the person's ideas on this may change through the process.

Psychiatrists have traditionally trained as medical doctors and then specialised in mental issues. The idea that not everything is curable by an appropriate treatment, particularly as the behaviourist school was pushed aside by the humanists, gave them something of an identity crisis of their own. Meanwhile, there has always been a popular caricature of the psychoanalyst, following ideas based on the teachings of Freud, as a bespectacled man with a terrible Austrian accent, sitting next to his client lying on a couch.

The important error in both these examples is the idea that the professional will provide a cure, or at least a solution. Moreover the client is very much in the power of the professional and, quite rightly, people do not like to lose control of their lives.

The account of counselling, given previously, dealt very much with practical issues and feelings in the present. Many TVs and TSs have had a rough ride through childhood, often with stories of rejection, one way or another. Such present-centred counselling may well acknowledge such past events and the way they affect the present. One's present cognitive interpretation may be re-evaluated, and one's schemata may be amended as they exist in the present.

Psychotherapy, on the other hand, involves actually working with those past issues in the hope of re-evaluating the cognitive interpretation that occurred then. The confronting and re-living of the past in this way, is often heavy going at first, possibly touching on the deepest emotions.

The counselling relationship is founded on absolute trust. It will only work if one really wants it to but, if one is prepared to release one's deepest feelings and fears, one may have a completely new outlook on life, with the confidence to solve some, if not all, of one's problems.

It may, of course, produce new ones, or give unexpected results, but the result is likely to be a feeling of empowerment, the feeling that life is on the right track, and that one is in control of it.

Many TSs, especially, complain about unhelpfulness from their consultant, but I feel that if they had spent some time taking in-depth general counselling, and confronted the issues, they would find the consultant more helpful.

Psychoanalysis or counselling therapy of this kind may, bearing in mind that the issues may reach back to babyhood, may take some years. The result is likely to be that the person simply finds confirmation that he needs to express his emotions in the way that he is already doing and, anyhow, he enjoys it.

Could the transvestite, perhaps, merge his feelings into a single schema, preferably without the need to cross-dress? It has to be said that understanding feelings does not always make them go away.

Reminding ourselves about what was said at the beginning of this chapter, people's gender schemata go back to the first few months of their lives. To change the very bases of them may mean re-evaluating their whole cognitive structure. Can people change their whole lives in such a drastic way?

Such a result of therapy may, be unexpected and wholly unwelcome. The TV may have built his whole life around a very macho persona. Can someone in a very masculine and aggressive career become gentle and nurturing? The TV's wife may see him as a very masculine man and not want someone more gentle in his approach to life.

Just as we don't know how many TVs there are, so we don't know how many have given up. After all, they wouldn't say so publicly, for they would want to keep their options open. In general, though, the real question is, "What distinguishes the happy TV from one that is consumed with such guilt and distress that it interferes with his ability to work and relate effectively?" What we wear and what we feel is only a problem because we see it as a problem. It obscures the fact that transvestism may be a natural and self-therapeutic reaction to social pressures, rather than an individual pathology. In the end, when we become who we really are, then we don't have to apologise to anyone.

Relatively Speaking
Diana Aitchison

I was asked, in 1989, if I would run the Beaumont Society's Wives and Partners Helpline known as WOBS, Women of the Beaumont Society. Within days of the new dedicated phone number being circulated I was inundated with calls from wives, partners and family members anxious to have someone understanding of their situation that they could talk to. We have now come to refer to them collectively as Significant Others. Many callers are just ringing up for practical advice having come to terms and accepted transvestism in a person whom they may describe as loving, caring and gentle. Others have found that this description does not fit their loved one and they are at a loss as what to do to alleviate a distressing situation. Often callers are totally ignorant of any facts concerning transvestism/cross dressing and wish to learn about the subject.

Common questions that are frequently asked such as "Is he gay?" or "Will he want the operation?" have been swelled by images culled from such diverse programmes as Coronation Street, Kilroy and the awful Jerry Springer Show. Little wonder that Significant Others are confused. The U.S. portrays transvestites as sexually driven drag queens, or gay transsexuals working in the sex industry whereas in the U.K. we are at pains to point out that most transvestites are nothing like this at all. The answers to most of these questions are relatively straightforward and have been covered elsewhere in this book. It is worth remembering too, that different Significant Others have different perspectives about their relationship with a crossdresser.

A wife or partner who considers herself reasonably tolerant of difference in others, suddenly finds that the situation is somewhat different when it concerns her own situation. After discovering a difference in her husband, the acronym 'nimby' takes on a new relevance and she may be shaken and disturbed by the strength of her hostility now that she too is the wife or partner of a man who needs to wear women's clothes occasionally. What was fine, OK, acceptable, fun as a student newly discovering an exciting hidden world that their parents might be shocked at was one thing but then it was a room mate who cross dressed and that was different. It seemed so harmless then.

To be told that, "After all, women can wear what ever they like. They've been wearing men's clothes for decades and no-one turns a hair, so why can't men?" can be infuriating to any woman. She recalls the hard-won freedoms for women so that they could ride a horse or bicycle appropriately clothed, operate machinery in munitions factories during the war or dig for victory as land-girls suitably dressed. All without wanting to be given a male name, grow a beard or pass as a man. The practicality of wearing those trousers then as now reflects the convenience of the garments for busy women's lifestyles. It has nothing to do with their gender identity. In fact they became the chosen fashion garments for women because they enhance a woman's femininity as well as giving her a less vulnerable image. Skirts and dresses have their place too of course in a birth gender woman's wardrobe, either as a uniform for work or for socialising or simply because she prefers them.

There is still a stigma among more traditional females who worry that trousers etc on women represent lesbianism, or they may believe that some men simply do not fancy women who wear trousers. It is this most traditional group of women who may be the most angered and distressed at the prospect of men wearing women's clothes. They are still being taught today that men value women for their vulnerability and femininity which will be a perfect foil for 'Mr. Right' when he comes along with all his healthy masculine, heterosexual and totally normal appetites. There may never have been a divorce in her family (still also stigmatised, you make your bed and you lie on it) and she may be too ashamed to admit to herself or her family that 'her man' is different. Sadly, she may find herself being a 'victim' to her crossdressing spouse's needs unless she develops a level of assertiveness and addresses the situation realistically. Some transvestites consciously or not may believe that if they choose a more submissive partner they can manipulate her into acceptance more easily than a street-wise socially aware woman. Unfortunately they are most likely to inflict psychological damage on her and will lose her anyway.

By the same token trouser wearers may suffer pangs of guilt that, somehow, how they dress is what has caused their loved one to adopt a cross-gender response by preferring female clothes for himself. She may have even been accused of being 'the cause' but this is not a true explanation. A man who has chosen to deny his transvestism at the onset of a relationship and who truly believes that he has got it under control, is often surprised and shocked by the sudden return of the feelings once he is living around all things female. Watching his wife or partner putting on her make-up for instance can bring to the surface all those hidden desires that he has been at such pains to hide. Angry and confused he perceives that it is her 'fault' for providing the trigger (albeit, totally innocently) that undoes all his hard work in suppressing his needs. With his secret exposed he panics, totally forgetting that his needs started when he was much younger, thus trying to avoid the criticism that invariably follows: "Why didn't you tell me before we married/lived together?"

Some mothers may have been aware that their son was 'borrowing' clothes and make up from his sisters, or indeed herself from quite a young age. Often they have chosen to ignore it hoping that he will grow out of it. Most, though, have been totally unaware off it until told that their burly, rugby playing, offspring, married with children, has come out as a transvestite, either by the son himself or, often, by an irate and tearful daughter-in-law. This can be a difficult time for all concerned with accusations sometimes being thrown. "It must be your fault, not a good wife are you?" "He says you always wanted a girl – you never wanted him!" Fathers may join in with "I said you were too soft with him, now look what you've done" Hopefully, given time and a willingness to talk, all parties will combine, along with siblings, to learn about the errant son/brother/husband.

Many couples prefer to see cross-dressing as a private pastime while others decide eventually to seek out a support group. Hostile wives are adamant that they want nothing to do with the transvestism and husbands are left to go it alone either confined to one room at home, or by opting to join a group. Here they can participate occasionally in confidential and safe surroundings with others in a similar situation. The relationship can still work very well as long as the boundaries are observed and each respects the other's space. Probably the greatest difficulty here is if the transvestite feels compelled to shave his legs and/or his body in order to appear more feminine when dressed, and to facilitate more success at 'passing' as a woman. Women generally dislike this obvious indicator of his female side and may become morose or even paranoid about losing sight of his masculinity or, equally, they may be fearful that others, such as their children, may notice his smooth, unmanly limbs. Her innate heterosexually-driven instincts may rebel at sleeping beside someone who, while attempting to behave like a heterosexual man, nevertheless smells and feels like a woman. He may become depressed that this important toiletry is denied him and tensions can build to enormous proportions until a compromise is reached. This often takes the form of no shaving in the summer to accommodate holidays, days on the beach or at the swimming pool and barbecues where shorts are obligatory for both genders but only the women have smooth hairless legs. However the onset of Autumn, shorter evenings and the long dark nights of Winter can herald a new outbreak of hostilities as he stocks up on razor blades and shaving cream for the duration. Again, compromises are sought. Thick tights (or two pairs of finer ones) or black, black stockings (only a transvestite can dream, drool and fantasise over these incredibly uncomfortable garments) can be one rather begrudging solution. Wives might give in over the underarm shaving, as no-one but her is going to see his bare oxters anyway, in a climate that rarely encourages this level of exposure before June. (No cheating by demanding that Christmas be spent in Benidorm). Shaving the genital area is generally a 'no-no' and jolly uncomfortable to boot.

Whether a wife or partner is hostile, tolerant or fully accepting depends on many finite considerations. A woman who has been brought up in the heartlands of masculine/feminine, clearly defined roles and attitudes, will feel that, to adopt a more liberal point of view to gender differences, may result in her being excluded by her peer group. "What will people think?" is an oft-used phrase even today. Its value has always been as a form of social control within families – for instance when one member wants to visibly dress or behave (punk, Teddy boy etc) in a way that brings unwanted attention on the family as a whole. Religion and culture will play an important role too in her struggle to accept the unacceptable; especially when deep down she wants her husband or partner to be happy and feels that he really shouldn't be denied the opportunity. She is therefore highly aware of the social phobias that exist in communities and is fearful of a community backlash.

Of course she may simply hate the whole concept and feel ill at the thought of ever seeing her husband or partner in an even remotely feminine role or image. Even his body language can infuriate her. The way that he holds a cup or cigarette, his habit of crossing his legs when seated or anything that is deemed female specific can cause her to reject him. She married/partnered a MAN not a Woman and that's that. Banning the behaviour totally 'or else' simply serves to drive her husband/partner underground where he resorts to secret, compulsive sorties into a bag of hurriedly acquired charity shop cast-offs, often disposing of them afterwards lest they be found, then the circle starts again when the next precious opportunity arises.

Parents and siblings are also very conscious of other peoples' perceptions concerning their son or brother. It is interesting that a girl can be viewed as a feisty tomboy if she adopts male traits, as it is generally understood that she will grow out of it. Only when a gender dysphoric girl grows up and repels all things feminine will the family generally start to worry. Their first thoughts will often be that their beloved daughter is lesbian, something which may cause them great anguish or simply be accepted as an explanation for the chosen lifestyle. The thought that their daughter may feel that she is a man trapped in a woman's body is frequently as devastating to them as it is if it is a son who is so afflicted. Women however are rarely transvestite in the sense that men are. It is fair to say that women generally have more space to live a cross role lifestyle than men, particularly in the area of what they wear, so women are better equipped nowadays to take on night classes in car maintenance for instance without raising an eyebrow. It is only the truly gender dysphoric woman who responds to the need to undertake radical surgery in order to live a fulfilled and honest existence, something that most of us take for granted.

Generally levels of acceptance can be achieved gradually where a transvestite is willing to see the situation through the eyes of those near and dear to him. Nobody is denying that his feelings about himself are strong and genuine and for life. However if they take a selfish and obsessive turn they will only serve to alienate those around him. Most relationships fail at this hurdle – no wife wants to feel that she is second best to a pseudo-woman who models on her, spends more time and money on the cross-dressing than on his wife and children, home or any important domestic obligation. Similarly, excessive time spent surfing the Internet for 'tranny' sites and chat rooms at the expense of a varied and regular social life that can be shared with the family is viewed as extremely unreasonable.

There is one group in particular who must come first in a transvestite's considerations and that is his children. If a man who cross-dresses chooses to marry and expresses a desire to be a regular husband and father, he must therefore put these responsibilities before his own needs. If he has done so his wife may well feel less threatened by his obsessiveness and feel that she can respond to his request for space and understanding more easily. She may insist though that it be kept well clear of the children so that they can grow up without any confusion about their father's gender identity. They may see him as a 'new man' hoovering away or doing the washing up and feel proud that their father is such an accommodating and modern human being, but not if he is wearing stockings and stilettos. Nevertheless, it is believed by a growing number of couples that it is better not to have secrets from the children. If Dad's needs are explained in a warm and loving way they can learn about gender differences as they are growing up, instead of possibly being confronted with an 'awful truth' when adult, as often happens. Many young people ring the Helpline to talk about their father's cross-dressing and are often furious that the knowledge has been denied to them throughout their childhood.

The fact that there was a 'secret' which may have put a great deal of stress on their parents, and therefore themselves, when they could have known about it, and saved all the anguish, is sometimes seen as condescending from the children's point of view. Many will concede, though, that their parents were only trying to protect them and, in time, they may come to accept this. If (as is sometimes the case) there is any suspicion that the children may have caught a glimpse of Dad wearing something inappropriate then it is better that parents are truthful with their children rather than lying about it. If the facts are presented in a matter-of-fact way most children take them on board uncritically and calmly. Ideally this should be done with both parents present and in agreement. This should not be used as an excuse however for a transvestite father to dress all the time, as the children still need to have plenty of 'man' time with him. They don't really want to hear that "Daddy can't take you to football this week as he has bought a new dress that he wants to try on." Children first, cross-dressing in moderation should be the cardinal rule.

Any transvestite who tries to force his needs on any Significant Other whether it is his wife, partner, parents or even best friend, will soon be viewed as selfish and arrogant and may find himself being rejected or even ejected from the household or social group. Men who feel that they are dual-role transvestites and who value a varied social life in their alter-ego would be better to find a group that accommodates this particular life style rather than trying to incorporate it into family life. How often do we hear on the Helpline "He wants his cake and eat it"? Egotism is a transvestite's worst enemy if he is not single and free to be as he likes. Here couples can be guided by their personal preferences in the matter. Many wives can come to be totally accepting and revel in the wide social life available to them through the various organisations that exist in Britain. Many are not the hedonistic dens of iniquity that most imagine them to be. Carefully chosen, they can be a source of great comfort and support both for the transvestite and his Significant Others. Even tolerant but cautious Significant Others (offspring, siblings and the odd mum can sometimes be found accompanying 'their' tranny as supporter) can benefit from an occasional foray into this alternative form of socialising. The more someone learns about gender differences the more at ease they become and in the case of wives and partners there is the added bonus of finding other wives and partners to talk things over with. She will learn about what is generally acceptable and what isn't and how other women handle the various obstacles to marital happiness.

Finally, what about the love life? This is a ticklish and often embarrassing area for callers to venture into yet it is usually at the crux of their difficulties. Understandably most women are not responsive to what they perceive as 'lesbian overtures' if they are firmly heterosexual themselves. Sometimes a woman has surprised herself to discover that she has in fact hidden lesbian/bisexual tendencies and is gratified that she can act these out with a responsive and truly grateful partner. For the most part though, women find that they cannot adapt their sexuality and transvestite men must accept and respect this fact. Changing one's sexuality unwillingly is as unnatural as being forced to change one's gender identity in order to suit someone else's needs, just as we now know that forcing some one to use their right hand, when they are left handed, is cruel and barbaric, as well as psychologically damaging. Yet, there was a time when forcing 'handedness' onto a child for social reasons was considered the 'norm' and in the 'bad old days' men viewed women as their chattel and property with whom they could do as they wished. Hopefully society has moved on and can accept that if they want to be understood and respected for who they are, they must also respect others for who they are. If the issue of sexual perspectives threatens to destroy a relationship it should be discussed in terms of individual needs that cannot reasonably be met, rather in terms of 'right' and 'wrong'. A transvestite who in sheer frustration tells his wife or partner that she is a frigid, narrow-minded prude who should look on the Internet at all those sites of 'understanding' wives, is nothing but a bully who refuses to accept that everyone is different. Counselling can help couples who genuinely want to find a way to keep each other happy without resorting to emotional blackmail especially if they are keen to hold their family together so that their children can grow in a two-parent family.

Unfortunately too many transvestites have fallen victim to their fantasies and sometimes have difficulty in recognising the harsh realities of being partnered or married, with or without children. Transvestites often ring the Helpline to test out a scenario that they think their wife or partner will fall for. Usually they are far-fetched and devoid of any practical considerations such as just telling her the truth. Invariably they are immature, selfish and misogynistic ego trips that variously concern their own perceptions of women loving them enough to put up with anything. Yet there are many loving, considerate wholly grounded men who cross dress too and each one must be seen as an individual. Many deserve to be married, treated as ordinary men who happen to have 'something extra'. Others I'm afraid, should not hide behind the façade of partnered or married life in order to 'fool society' (their words not mine) and cover up their own shortcomings and weaknesses, so that they can be viewed as socially acceptable and respectable, while harbouring secret thoughts and fancies.

Ultimately couples who are trying to accommodate transvestism within their joint lifestyle really need to discuss everything calmly and matter-of-factly with the emphasis on truth and trust. No Significant Other should feel that they have no choice in what their loved one does. There is always room for compromises where everyone wants a happy and balanced outcome.

In the best of worlds men who have these needs really should open up to a new romantic interest as soon as reasonably possible, mindful of the fact that they can trust the person with the information. Here is an indicator of how suitable the person will be as a more permanent partner. If you can't trust them at the beginning, it is better not to say anything, and make a permanent exit from the situation, rather than risk being humiliated. Being friends and soul mates first can be the forerunner to an open and honest life bonding. Far too often transvestites feel that they must sweep someone off their feet in case they find out and leave, instead of honouring the old-fashioned virtue of really getting to know each other before making a commitment. Relying on his own powers of persuasion and devastating charm can only be a recipe for disaster and he will probably deserve everything he gets.

Coming Out

Help and Support for Transvestites

Jay Walmsley

The best help for a transvestite is another (sensible) transvestite. Better still are more transvestites. Equally, the best help for a transvestite's partner is another transvestite's partner, preferably more than one.

A transvestite needs the reassurance that what he is doing is not wrong. Most feel guilty in some way. Acceptance by others is often the necessary prelude to shedding that particular load. Meeting others, being accepted by others, becoming part of a social life with others, leads to a freedom and a pleasure that is quite unknown to the solitary closet transvestite.

This is equally true for wives and partners. Most are shocked when they discover the truth. Many cannot handle it but more than a few find the resources to stick by their man. After all there are worse things. The husband could be running loose with other women. He could be alcoholic, he could gamble the family cash away and he could beat wife and children. Transvestites, apart from their special need, are usually caring husbands. Therefore, if the wife can speak to another wife, compare notes and ideas, she may find a way, usually over several months, to come to terms with the situation. It is often the case that the special honesty and intimacy then in the relationship can enhance it wonderfully.

How does one obtain help? The best step is to telephone one of the helplines. These exist to help transvestites, transsexuals, their partners and families and anyone interested. They are 'manned' by experienced volunteers and the caller may always remain entirely anonymous,

The **Beaumont Trust** runs an excellent service, nationally. Call 07000 287878 on a Tuesday or a Thursday evening between 7 and 11 pm to be in touch with a volunteer. They do not offer detailed counselling but will give whatever practical advice and reassurance is needed. The call is made in complete security and names or any personal particulars are not sought or necessary. The volunteer has a list of available national and local societies and will be only too pleased to give the appropriate telephone numbers or addresses that will help. For those who would prefer to write, the address is Beaumont Trust, BM CHARITY, London WC1N 3XX.

The **Beaumont Society** is the largest national society. It provides an excellent magazine and has a network of Regional and Area Officers throughout the country. They will meet with members and newcomers and offer a welcome and advice. Many organise social functions in their area. The society itself organises weekends, usually involving taking over an entire hotel for a weekend so that members may dress and attend dinners, social functions etc in complete freedom. To obtain details write to Beaumont Society, 27, Old Gloucester Street, London WC1N 3XX or ring the Beaumont Trust (no connection) helpline for Regional Officers' contact numbers.

The third body is the **Seahorse Society** which is centred in the South. A small friendly society, it has a good newsletter and may be reached via the Beaumont Trust helpline or by writing direct c/o BM Seahorse, London WC1N 3XX

The **Northern Concord,** is a totally voluntary organisation based in Manchester. It meets every Wednesday night throughout the year, with an average attendance of forty to sixty people. It meets in a city centre bistro and provides changing facilities, hot and cold meals and many social functions. It produces its own excellent magazine *Cross Talk,* which is available to non-members. To contact them, please write to Northern Concord, PO Box 258, Manchester M60 1LN.

Throughout the British Isles, there are local groups, both large and small, often meeting in community centres, sometimes supported by their Local Authorities. Since names, numbers and addresses change from time to time, the reader is advised to refer to the Beaumont Society's magazine, or the Beaumont Trustline.

For partners and wives there is a helpline **Women of the Beaumont Society** Regional phone numbers can be obtained from the Beaumont Society or the Beaumont Trust.

What goes on at these meetings in all these groups? What do they do? What can a highly nervous newcomer expect?

Firstly, a warm welcome. Everyone has been new once and understands. Secondly security. Everyone has some sort of security problem and confidentiality is vital. All that is needed of a newcomer is a femme name and a place of origin e.g. Shirley from Purley.

Thirdly usually a social get-together which enables members to meet and talk about whatever they want. A newcomer will always find practical help and advice. Wives and partners and indeed family members are always welcome and more than a few usually are present.

The meetings are usually a big disappointment to any one seeking high jinks. The usual comparison is with a Women's Institute meeting and this is pretty accurate. The detached observer would merely see a lot of women chatting together over a cup of tea or perhaps something stronger.

They do offer that companionship with others who know your feelings, have been through what you have been through, and who care about others. A newcomer can obtain much help and information. Inevitably he will grow in confidence, become more capable, make excellent friends and quickly find that transvestism can be a great pleasure and deeply fulfilling.

Coming Out
Jed Bland

There are a number of social groups listed in this book which offer postal membership, and regular newsletters with, usually, systems for communicating with other members. It is emphasised that this is not for purpose of finding sexual partners. They all have to assume that, if you are married, that your partner agrees that you should approach them and, if you are under eighteen, that you are contacting them with the permission of your parents or guardians. They all have a strict code of security. To other members you will only be known by your 'femme name' and your membership number, unless you choose otherwise. Any correspondence will be completely confidential.

Most people begin this way, and find it enough to simply communicate by post. However, sooner or later, most want to meet others in person. Up to date details of local meetings can be found in the newsletters already mentioned, and it is perfectly acceptable for one to 'dip one's toe' in the water by attending in one's everyday male clothes. It is left to the individual to choose when, and if, he wishes to appear as his female self and, for those who feel unable to travel 'en femme', changing facilities are usually provided. Again, no-one need know anything about your everyday life. Even if you did meet someone you know, as I did, you have to remember that they have just as much to hide as you do.

Everyone attending their first meeting is entering unknown territory. They may make a dozen false approaches, and may hang around outside for an hour working up their nerve. Then they take a deep breath, and metaphorically shutting their eyes, plunge in through the door.

The First Time

Jenny Baker
The Northern Concord

Remember your first visit to a group meeting? The fear, the terror, the panic . . .
"Somebody might see me, that I know!"
"What should I say?"
"Are these people alright?"
"Will the world cave in on me?"
"It's not worth it. I'll try again next week!"

Recognise any of these? The realisation that you are not the only person in the world that cross-dresses. And yet, because of the guilt people are made to feel, the uncertainty . . .
"If all these other people are doing it, are they guilty as well. Should I really be mixing with them, let alone socialising?"

And then you are inside . . .
"Have I done the right thing?"
"Think of an excuse to leave."
"Take deep breaths. Don't panic!"
"What's wrong with these people. They act as though it were perfectly normal to walk about in women's clothes. Perhaps they don't have as much to lose as me?"

Then gradually, as the adrenalin dissipates itself, the slow dawning that . . .

"Well, perhaps this wasn't such a bad idea after all."

"It's quite exciting really."

"What, time to go already?"

"Are we here again next week?"

"Great, see you then."

"I've done it! Unbelievable. Who would have thought somebody like me, in my personal circumstances, would end up doing something like this, with a bunch of complete strangers."

"Must get down earlier next week. What a nice gang of people."

Passing
Jay Walmsley

To 'pass' means to be able to dress as a woman and to mingle with others who do not know you without being recognised as a man. To be 'read' means that someone sees through your illusion.

To pass needs a great deal of hard work. It involves clothes, shoes, make-up, hair, accessories, voice and deportment. It all has to be right, down to the last little detail. That means a lot of studying women, practice, trial and error and more practice and study.

The best help is of course to have a supportive female. Failing that membership of a group is very helpful. With no support you will have to do it on your own. Read *Style Made Simple* by Janet Impey, a Women's Institute handbook available in book stores. There is masses of practical wisdom in a small volume.

Clothes. If you are a standard size, you simply buy them from dress shops. Men buy clothes for women or themselves frequently. Shop assistants simply do not bother. Select what you want and pay for it. You will have to select style, cut, length, colour to suit yourself and it will take a while to get it right. Trial and error comes in here. There are outsize shops, Evans and special departments that can help really big people and Long Tall Sally is the only small chain of shops for really tall women, 5 foot 8 and over. Don't neglect underwear. The proper underpinnings are vital and a good girdle will eliminate any unfortunate bulges. Libraries offer good books on women's clothes and should not be neglected.

Shoes are often harder. All stores offer women's sizes up to 8 which can be selected off the shelf. Some shops go up to

9. Try Saxone for up to 12. After that you are best advised to seek help from your local group.

Makeup. Again the local libraries do offer good books on the subject. Read them and save money. Think about your colouring and needs and buy accordingly. Most chemists and stores have racks of cosmetics where you can browse and buy. Trial and error and much practice are necessary. Think about all the practice young girls undertake. For beard cover, a good foundation with a close shave is essential. If the beard growth is heavy, camouflage creams are available.

Hair. There are specialist wig sellers which are well worth patronising. Most are happy to help transvestites in confidence and will give you the best advice and value. Failing them, most department stores have a wig department where you can buy off the shelf. Buy a shade close to your own so that it looks natural and of a length and style suitable to your years and image.

Accessories. You will need a handbag, ideally matching your shoes and going with your clothes. A good leather one repays the investment and will last. An old worn bag always looks more realistic than a new one. Learn to carry it like a woman. Good leather belts are always an investment and you need scarves and handkerchiefs, to your taste and style. Jewellery is vital and should be used to help disguise bad features and enhance good ones.

Voice. Practice a soft voice, speaking from the roof of the mouth and not from the stomach. Always, always, always let someone see you before you speak. They can accept a wrong voice if they think you are a woman but not if you speak before they see you.

Deportment. Move, act, be like a woman at all times. Don't mince or camp or exaggerate but be feminine, not masculine. Only observation and trial and error will help here.

The difference is hard to define but easy to see and this is where most go wrong. Practice till it hurts.

Most importantly, you can dress as glamorously as you wish for transvestite meetings. It won't do, however, for passing in public. Look around you. Most women dress down most of the time. It might be a waste of possibilities, but it is reality. Most of the time, women haven't the time or energy to bother to dress up. Sorry, but if you want to pass, you have to look no different.

When you have got it right, and be really sure that you have, comes the time to put yourself to the test. There is nothing so nerve wracking as the first time you appear dressed in public. You imagine all eyes are on you but if you have done your job properly, they won't be. Go purposefully about your business, women don't dillydally. Go really in public, e.g. a shopping centre. With so many people to look at, they won't concentrate on you. However do bear in mind that people look closely at women whereas men are never scrutinised. That takes some getting used to.

Don't go out at night in dark areas. It may feel safe, nothing may happen, but it's risky. It is unlikely that anyone will beat you up in a supermarket in broad daylight. Finding you alone on a dark night, young thugs may think it a pleasure.

Avoid young hooligans. Young people are the quickest to read you, particularly young girls. However most people, if they do read you, apart from the initial surprise, will not bother. The great British reserve, and the wish not to be involved, is on your side. However young hooligans have nothing to lose. Baiting you could be their idea of fun. Avoid such situations. Don't get into tight corners, and avoid pubs on your own.

Confidence is vital. If you look confident and natural, you pass. Nervousness shows and people wonder what you have to be nervous about. Confidence is hard to acquire and does not remain constant day to day. Some days are not as good as others. Avoid getting flustered. Remember all the practice you have done and how you ought to look.

However, if you have got everything right, you should pass undetected. It is a wonderful feeling. There you are, just another woman in the great mass of people. You are you and nobody knows. Enjoy it. After all that work, you deserve it.

The Joy of Transvestism
Danielle (S4458)

When asked "What's it like to wear the most beautiful dresses in the world?" Elizabeth Hurley, film actress, producer and one time cosmetics model, said "Heavenly!"

That's how I feel about putting on beautiful feminine clothes too. It's a drug-free form of Ecstasy! But in its own way, cross-dressing is equally addictive! "Heavenly" is not a strong enough word!

This valuable book is full of helpful advice, all of it to be studied carefully and absorbed by you and yours as appropriate to your circumstances. But in my view one thing is missing from most sections of this erudite publication:

Transvestism is Fun! Enjoyment! A Delight! A JOY!

It is the male-to-female cross-dresser for whom this book is most intended. At least, that's what I would have thought and expected from any book titled 'Transvestism' and mostly it's true. Comment on other aspects of Gender Dysphoria should be included but not covered in depth. I know that many of the authors of other sections of this book are deeply involved in full transsexualism in one way or another, so I hope this chapter will act as a bit of an antidote to their too-close-to-TS perceptions.

I am not personally totally aware what inspires the rarer female-to-male cross-dresser, but I do know from discussions with a few of them that the end result is much the same – it's an activity that gives personal happiness, delight, some thrills and perhaps a perceived joyful freedom from what might seem the unwritten limitations of the female world.

Although many of the issues might also apply to full-time transgenderists and transsexuals, their eventual motivation is not totally the same as for we TVs. In any case they have several serious books on their specific issues (I recommend *Gendys Guide to Transsexualism, Transgenderism and Gender Dysphoria*, ISBN 0 9525107 2 3, from BM Gendys, London WC1N 3XX).

Dressing up is a physical pleasure.

Remember all the fun we had dressing up as children? Cowboys and Indians, Doctors and Nurses, Halloween spectres? This is how your transvestism should be now - something to throw yourself into with imaginative joy in an almost childlike way, to be the TV you want to be. Otherwise - what's the point?

How do you get the courage? By appreciating what you could be and by making your dreams come true as best you can. Joy should be involved in every aspect of your cross-dressing - not anxiety and terror! Yes, I know but you can read the doom and gloom bits and about how to deal with them elsewhere in these pages.

Once you begin dressing up, enjoy every part of it! How many times do you get a chance to indulge in your womanhood? Make the most of these special occasions, especially if they are infrequent.

Appreciate the beauty of your shimmering silver satin dress and matching eye make up. Drip about in glorious jewellery and Miss Dior perfume. Enjoy the moment!

You have to put effort, dedication, enthusiasm, skill and yes - lust - into it. Cross-dressing is a physical shot in the arm (and it's no wonder that for many it can lead to a strong need for some self-applied sexual relief!) Dressing up makes you feel better. You know you look so good - and often much younger too.

Cross-dressing's also about exuberance. Success comes with making an effort to create whatever feminine illusion you fancy. It gives you the means to express your moods and whims - your chance to make a personal statement. It's about exploring a world of clothes otherwise not normally available to you in your regular daily grind. It's about overcoming some life-nurtured no-go's on a personal basis. It's about becoming a totally different and more compelling you! It's about making your dreams come true - the reality of putting yourself into various feminine roles, even if that sometimes leads into areas of dress fetishism. Holding onto those dreams and stepping beyond them becomes an additional pleasure in itself.

The joyous desire to cross-dress undoubtedly gets stronger for most transvestites the more we practice it. For most of us it becomes a compulsion - something almost always at the forefront of our minds. I admit cross-dressing can become even obsessive - something we do need to guard against if there are those unavoidable domestic, business and social limitations we all encounter.

I can't imagine dressing up for anything BUT pleasure! It's the same for real women too. It pleases me in the way nothing else does. There are many other joys in life - the love of a good woman (for a TV they have to be especially good) and of the family, of enjoyable and profitable employment (for some), of sex in all its forms, and/or of whatever sport or pastime turns you on. But when I go out dressed, the adrenaline pump gives me a high beyond them all - and one that lasts for several hours if not a day or two. In any case I can do some of my favourite things at the same time as I'm dressed! Double the pleasure!

Remember here, I am writing as a TV - not a TG or a TS, for whom feminine clothes are an everyday norm.

First of all you have to prepare yourself. This may involve bathing, de-hairing, rubbing in nice smelling creams, and spritzing yourself with deodorants or with a fantastically sensual and delightful perfume.

Then the excitement builds as you go through the exquisite pain of deciding what to wear. Much of the pleasure of cross-dressing comes in this planning process. Selecting (having already enjoyed the thrill of going out to buy them) glamorous clothes that are not included in a man's world is part of the joy, even when (frustratingly) you can't make up your mind what to wear - how very female!

Having finally decided (or not) you perhaps start your joyous evening or weekend *en femme* with a bra or corset, a girdle, roll-on or knickers, or perhaps a corselette. You slip into some tights or stockings. This is often a good moment to get into a pair of strappy sandals, dainty shoes or knee-length boots, any of which may be high heeled and all of which are overtly feminine apparel (this way you won't ladder your stockings on a misplaced carpet tack). There are several moments of intimate joy here for every TV.

Into the bust area you slip those lovely silky-soft pliable prostheses, which droop convincingly into the bra cup. They are cold, but soon begin to warm to your body. As you move, they move with you.

You can hardly wait to sit at your dressing table and apply your cosmetics - foundation, blush, eye makeup, maybe false eyelashes or mascara, finishing powder and lipstick.

Those of you (most of us), without your own golden locks, tug on a wig cap (or you should) and slide your favoured postiche onto your head - this is the moment when you see in the mirror that magic moment when a bloke in cosmetics becomes truly and joyously feminine. If the wig is shoulder-length or longer, the swish of hair across your bare shoulders is a completely female and (I find) a compelling sensation.

Finally you are ready for the pleasure of slipping into your outer clothes. A flowing floral dress, perhaps, or a PVC or leather mini skirt and boob tube? An off-the-shoulder ball gown, a smart power suit or a complete country girl outfit? Then it's that feminine outer garment – a faux fur collared long coat, a bomber jacket, or perhaps a sexy mac? And for those special occasions – maybe – a big hat? Having a hat-net over your face is another unique female experience – and one not to be missed.

Then it's off to whatever event is your particular entertainment. Perhaps an evening at your local TV club? Perhaps you and your SO are going shopping together for those female garments that it's hard to do, on your own, as a man? Trying on big hats in a department store, for example (I have never plucked up the nerve to do that in male drag).

I admit there's not so much joy in taking it all of again at the end of the day – but you can compensate a bit by retiring in a gorgeous nightie or satin pyjamas.

For me, if I may write personally for a moment, the ultimate garment is the wedding dress, complete with accessories and veil. There cannot be anything more totally feminine than that? (I have it written into my will that I want to go to my Maker in one, so I will be thus dressed for eternity). But that's just my personal choice. There are many thousands of other feminine delights you can try.

Whatever is your bag – all I would ask of any TV is that, whatever style you choose, dress to the best standard that your circumstances and ability allow. Wherever you go inside or outside the TV scene – there's far worse than you out there!

You can dress boringly if you want – it's your choice – and there are lots of good fashion books to tell you how to do so. And don't ignore the advice elsewhere in this book which adds up to saying, quite correctly, that there are many occasions when it is *wise* to do so. You can compensate then by wearing, for your own pleasure, the nicest lingerie you own underneath.

But when London or Hollywood society gets dressed up - everyone loves it! The designer clothes on display are so beautiful. As Liz Hurley said - "Heavenly!"

So like the big stars I say "Give 'em something to remember you by!" And give yourself something to remember you by too, whilst you are at it! Make your dressing up a gala event - especially if you can't get to do it too often. We all need *joie de vivre* in our lives - without it life is boring.

To your own self be true. You are not if the things you want to do or have (in any sphere) do not give you a sense of joy and a lot of fun. Life needs to be full of pleasurable activities, maybe to compensate for the work you do (should you not enjoy it) and/or the responsibilities you and I necessarily have.

I claim there's nothing more joyful, pleasurable, and harmless (except to your credit cards) than being a tranny!

Now you can go and read the more boring bits elsewhere in this tome knowing your tranny life will be filled with JOY!

Books mentioned in this chapter.

Guide to Transsexualism, Transgenderism and Gender Dysphoria. Alice Purnell (1998) Gendys Network, BM GENDYS, London WC1N 3XX

Into The Open
Jed Bland

Coming out starts with discovery, confession or speaking to a counsellor or phoneline. It goes on until the person has found a state of being with which he is content. Usually there has to be a compromise, and it is often a long process. Some of this book so far has been heavy going, and some of it may have struck uncomfortably close to home.

While it ends the secrecy and the loneliness, there are still problems to be considered. Firstly there is a limit to who one can tell. Even though the transvestite's wife may, up to a point, be willing to accept the fact of her husband's cross dressing, she may be very averse to neighbours and relatives knowing about it.

As Carolyn put it, in theNorth Western Gender Alliance's newsletter: *"It is a very lonely experience not being able to talk about one of the most fulfilling and extraordinary parts of my life with the people I see everyday, including my closest friends. I can never stop feeling shame about being a crossdresser if I must keep it secret from everyone except other crossdressers."*

Then there are the person's work colleagues. Recently, BBC's *One Life* documentary series featured a transvestite from Sutton in Ashfield in North Derbyshire. When the facts of her crossdressing became known, she was sacked by the District Council for whom she worked. Recent legislation protects transsexual people regardless of whether they have started to live full time in their new role or not, or whether they have undergone any reassignment surgery or not.

However, this legislation has not, so far, been extended to transvestites. One might think that, if a person was not planning to appear at her workplace in anything other than her male role, what she did in her own time was entirely her own business, particularly if it did not affect her ability to do her job. In the real world, whatever the issues of this particular case, even if she wins her appeal to an Industrial Tribunal, employers have many subtle ways of making life unpleasant for those they take a dislike to.

Consequently there are limits to the changes one can make to one's appearance, such as shaping one's eyebrows, or shaving one's arms and legs during Summer. One somewhat extreme solution, of course, might be to take up a sport such as competitive cycling or swimming.

Just as with anyone finding a new hobby, the new freedom may bring a round of over-indulgence, with cross dressing at every opportunity, and a fortune spent on clothing and petrol visiting every available meeting. Quite reasonably, the transvestite's wife may resent so much time being spent that is not shared with the family.

Where there are children, it may not be acceptable to even keep clothes in the home, which may be the reason many change at the meeting, or store their clothes at a friend's home and change there. The possibility of a breakdown or accident, while travelling en femme is another issue to consider.

The Police Are Only Human!
The Common Sense Approach In Dealing With The Police
By kind permission of Northern Concord.
First published in Cross Talk Magazine

The Officer who wrote the article says *"This article was written for publication in Northern Concord's magazine Cross Talk and prior to any published Police policies in relation to Transvestites or Transsexuals.*

It is intended as a streetwise guide to our community and in no way represented or purports to represent any policies of the police as a whole.

This is a police officer's own view on how you could, not should, but could be treated by other officers. The comments are as valid now as when the piece was written, the findings of the Stephen Lawrence enquiry; and the admission by Sir Paul Condon and David Wilmott of the Greater Manchester Police that racism is institutionalised within the police force confirm the possible attitudes you may encounter. After all, the article is titled 'The Police Are Only Human', and that means that societies opinions and attitudes are represented by police officers as well."

This article was written by a serving member of the British Police Force, i.e. direct from the constable's mouth as you might say. The information given is her personal perspective, hopefully a helpful guide to any encounters you may have with the boys and girls in blue.

Hello, my name's Jean and I've been asked as a serving policewoman to give you a view of your interest from my side of the fence. I'll try not to bore you with all the legal jargon, however I will attempt to give you an insight into some of the problems you may encounter, should you be unfortunate enough to be spoken to by one of my colleagues whilst you're out dressed in all your finery. I'll also try to explain the best way to react and the things you should and shouldn't do. A lot of it is just common sense. However, there are some points you may not be aware of.

Underneath our uniforms apart from various types of underwear, which we won't go into, is a human being. This person has the same emotional feelings, mental attitudes, likes and dislikes as any other average human being. In other words, the attitudes you come across in the police are as varied as in any job or profession.

We're actually trained to be unbiased and not to discriminate against anybody for their race, colour or gender or anything else come to that matter, but obviously the individual's personality will sometimes emerge, and bearing this in mind you'll come across a fairly wide spectrum of attitudes. I know fellow officers who would be helpful, some would definitely be amused and others, well, they would just be pig ignorant and intolerant.

The police force is very much a macho organisation and when confronted by yourselves, two or more officers would probably attempt to make witty comments to each other so that they wouldn't show whether they approve or not. I've heard them in the canteen talking about their encounters and most treat it as a humorous situation and laugh about it. There are the obvious comments from some officers of faggots, 'queers' etc, but these are similar comments as you would get from any cross section of the population.

The important thing to remember is that most of us are tolerant and are happy to let people get on with what they want to do, providing of course it's not upsetting anybody else.

This brings me to the legal aspects of cross dressing, if that's the right choice of phrase. The first thing to remember is that it is not an offence to dress in the attire of the opposite sex in public. The problems arise from the way other people behave towards you, and of course, how you behave yourself. Let's look at some situations you may come across

People Trouble

You're out walking about town dressed and you are hassled by a group of youths, a drunk, or some other bloody-minded individual. Should the person or group become excessively abusive towards you, it could end up with police intervention. As I've already mentioned, you are not committing any offence by dressing as a woman, but depending on how you act in the situation and the attitude of the officer attending, it could be construed that you, being dressed, has provoked the disturbance and as such a 'Breach of the Peace' has occurred

Breach of the Peace is the commonest offence that the police deal with on a day to day basis, and officers are not stupid despite what the tabloid press would have you believe, so it should be obvious upon his or her arrival that it's you who is the victim and not the perpetrator of the trouble.

You can help yourself here by approaching the officer first, explaining the situation. Be as helpful as possible, be polite, answer any questions. If you are calm and sensible despite the way you are dressed, his or her attention will be drawn to the other idiot! However, should you encounter one of my less tolerant colleagues, let me explain the procedure:

Should the attending officer decide that it's you that's the cause of the trouble, he has the following options.

a) He could ask you to leave the area.

b) He could escort you away from the area.

c) In the worst case he could arrest you.

If the officer chooses the last course of action you would be taken to the police station, where upon arrival you must give your correct name, date of birth and address, plus any other information required. Failure to provide your correct name means you will remain at the police station until your identity can be established.

Having given all your correct details you would be thoroughly searched, all monies and personal effects would be removed from you and booked into property. A breach of the peace is a straight forward process with no interview required. The officer would just complete the relevant forms. Remember that you are entitled to a solicitor, should you feel the need for one. If you don't know one yourself, you can ask to speak to the duty solicitor, free of charge. Breach of the Peace is one of the few offences that has no bail, because it's believed by the arresting officer that a breach of the peace would re-occur if you were allowed to return to the situation. This means that you would be detained overnight and would be taken before the Court in the morning, the crunch being that you would be dressed as you were arrested. Depending on your ability to pay, you would either be fined or serve a period in one of Her Majesty's hotels.

The previous scenario is not meant to put you off going out dressed by scaring you witless, but just to make you aware of the worst that can happen. Most police don't like arresting people for this offence, especially if the situation could be resolved in another way. Just bear in mind that if you are daft, it could happen to you.

Credit Cards

The next piece of advice I would like to give you is regarding the use of credit cards whilst out dressed. You may have gone to a lot of trouble to obtain a credit card in your femme name by deception, (This doesn't mean I'm saying TVs and TSs have any criminal intent, they just want the convenience of their own credit card whilst out dressed en femme), even though the card is registered against your own bank account. Think about it, if you do get 'read', the shopkeeper will see a man, dressed as a woman, trying to use a woman's credit card. Suspicious, I'm sure you'd agree. So who would they call? You've guessed it! The boys and girls in blue who would then have to investigate who you really are.

Cars

One of the most common dealings transvestites have with the police is probably whilst driving a car. It's very easy for everybody to help themselves here and ensure they don't get stopped in the first place. Firstly, make sure your car is 100% mechanically and electrically roadworthy, i.e. all your lights work, the exhaust is not hanging off etc. If your car appears normal and doesn't arouse the attention of the police in any other way, there is no reason for us to stop you. We'll pick on someone else, there's plenty of people about just asking us to stop them. The golden rule is don't attract attention, drive at the appropriate legal speed, drive sensibly, don't race amber lights and don't hog the road. All very simple common sense advice.

Let's now say you are stopped whilst you're driving a car. It's an offence not to give your name, address and date of birth. You also have to say who the keeper or owner of the car actually is. Now don't try to be clever here, remember by the time you've been stopped, in most cases the officer will already know who the car's registered owner actually is, having conducted a routine computer check over the radio. So don't, whatever you do, try giving a false name and address. Section 25 of the Police and Criminal Evidence Act allows him to arrest you and take you to the Police Station until he can verify who you are.

If your car is a company car, say so! Tell the officer who the company is, we won't phone them or inform on you. All we're trying to establish here is that the car is being driven by the person it's supposed to be driven by and not Billy the car thief.

If you have your correct documents with you (Driving Licence, Insurance Certificate, MOT) he may let you proceed on your way. If you don't have the relevant paperwork, he will give you a form to produce them within 7 days to a police station of your choice. If they are in order, that's the last you'll hear of it, if not, you could be summonsed to the Court. So the motto here is make sure your car's paperwork is all in order.

Drinking & Driving

I know this might sound like stating the obvious but under no circumstances even think about drinking and driving. Should you be found to be over the limit by the officer he would arrest you on the spot. You would be taken to the Police Station and if after providing a specimen, you are found to be over the limit, you would be charged and taken to Court. Whilst at the station you would have to undergo the humiliation of being searched and possibly mocked by one of my less thoughtful colleagues. Once charged, you would be fingerprinted, photographed and a computer record of your details created. This record would stay in existence until you die (unless the Court found you not guilty – then it would be destroyed along with the fingerprints)

Once you'd been fingerprinted and photographed, you would be released, but only after an officer had called at your home address to verify it. You wouldn't be allowed to collect your car until the following day or for at least several hours after the arrest. So don't drink and drive under any circumstances, it's just not worth it.

Finally, I'd just like to make the point that I haven't heard any officers wishing to make it a personal campaign to arrest transvestites. Most Police Officers are professionals and will only arrest in a situation in which they have no other option. No other option because that has been taken away by the nature of the offence or the pure stupidity of the individual. So please don't help create a situation in which you take those options away. And last but not least enjoy yourselves.

Footnote by the Editor
In these increasingly nervous times, it is just possible that the Police will stop and want to search you, particularly if you are travelling home late from a meeting. It has to be said that we know of no-one in the trans community that it has happened to, though around a million so-called 'stop and searches' are carried out each year. Generally it is if a crime has been committed or suspected, particularly involving drugs, stolen goods or terrorism.

The police have clearly defined rules that they must follow, and they are given training for dealing with minority groups such as transgender people. They must give a reason and it must be a good one, and identify themselves with warrant card, and the name of their station. You need not give your name and you are entitled to a written record.

They can search your outer clothing only. A strip search must be usually be carried out in the Police station and, in the worst case, intimate searches must be by a medical practitioner.

A Final Word
Jed Bland

It worries me that, though we give permission, and while this is necessary, it isn't sufficient, and it can cause as much trouble as it saves. Permission to have feelings implies the need to learn how to have them. To 'come out' too quickly may be as dangerous as not coming out at all. The TV newly 'out' has to find his own way and I am very much in favour of it happening together with a credible long term counselling relationship.

Many TVs have a macho reaction after their session as a 'female'. The further they go into the role, particularly if pushed, or led on, initially, by other thoughtless transvestites, the more extreme the reaction is likely to be. On two occasions, I have observed this to be extremely violent.

Somehow, they have to experience this other life that they have permission for, while keeping one foot in reality and not getting swept away in the fantasy. Once the initial nerves are over, there is a considerable amount of glamour involved in attending meetings and mixing with others.

Often there are transsexuals who are full of their plans for their changeover, and are sometimes very negative about people they label as fetishists. To the newcomer, they have a certain glamour; they are 'going all the way'. Many transvestites have been 'out' for so long that they have forgotten what it was like for newcomers. They may be very impatient of any reservations that the newcomer may have.

Sometimes, in building up the sexual daydream, some transvestites imagine themselves in a sexual relationship with a woman, others with a man. Usually, they have no detailed picture of their imaginary partner. They may develop the role further, and may explore it into an imagined relationship, without really thinking it through.

If the transvestite has started to think in terms of a relationship with a woman, in his female role, his wife is likely to be very upset by the idea that he wants a lesbian relationship.

From time to time, a transvestite speaks of his puzzlement about feelings of sexual attraction to men that he could not possibly contemplate if he were not 'dressed'. The idea that the transvestite first finds a different expression of himself, then builds a different persona and then may extend the make-believe into the exploration of the natural relationship for that role, would help in understanding the confusion of people in this position.

The TV may go to a meeting, simply to enjoy being a woman. At meetings where members of the public may be present, or in gay clubs, one of the ladylike things he has to learn is how to counter amorous advances in a tactful manner. Especially if he is young and attractive, he may be flattered by the attention, full of the freedom to portray the role and take it further than he intends to. Even though he may not want a sexual relationship, he is very much in the position of a young teenage girl, first discovering the power of her sexual attraction. Many men, both gay and 'straight', find transvestites a considerable 'turn-on'. He may meet another transvestite who is bisexual, or he may attract the attentions of gay man who, quite naturally, does not realise the true state of affairs. If a one night stand follows, there may be a call to the helpline, at four in the morning, from the TV needing to work through his shame and disgust at what has happened.

Some have suggested that we should not include these issues, but we believe they are important. It seems to us to be extremely patronising to regard wives as the 'little woman' to be metaphorically patted on the head and told everything will be alright. At the same time, forewarned is forearmed. The TV, aware of the possibility of this sort of chance encounter, of being 'swept away', may consider it more carefully. Moreover it is the scenario that worries AIDS workers the most.

It is important for people to decide why they want to do something and to be emotionally and practically prepared. A TV might well, in fact, decide that he does like men. The real question is not who turns you on, but who can you build a relationship with.

Conclusion

In exploring this whole new world of feelings, it is often obsessional at first, with an endless round of meetings, extravagant purchases of clothes and so on. In the end, an accommodation is found.

The transvestite phoning the helpline is full of the question "Why?" We hope that this book has given some clues. It's time, now, to look onwards and outwards. The important question is "What now?" What changes will he make to his life? For change has already happened. After the first step out of the closet there is no going back.

It's time to enjoy what is, after all, innocent and harmless enjoyment, providing it is done with sensitivity and consideration of those around him.

Will it change him as a person? To bring his 'gentle' side into his daily life as a man would change him so greatly that he might not be able to continue in his career, but he gains a clear idea of his male role, with the idea of being able to take a rest from it from time to time. In effect, he becomes a cross-dresser.

On the other hand, a friend of mine read this through, and said, "I don't think I could do that. Living my life swapping between roles." I respect that. Although she is attending a gender clinic, she regards herself, not as a transsexual, but as transgendered. She is also single.

In the end it depends on who you are, and what is valuable in your life. It may seem a cliché, but a great poet once wrote "To thine own self be true."

Dangerous Delusions
David Elvy

When I first co-wrote the article Dangerous Delusions, the terms HIV/AIDS and Gay were, in minds of most peoples synonymous. Some years further along we know that HIV is and never has been selective in terms of sexuality. We also know more about the spread of the disease on a worldwide basis. Formerly there always seemed to be reference to the USA as a source rather than as the country where it was first assessed in global terms. Now that limited vision has been shattered and HIV is seen not as a gay issue but an horrific world problem, being transmitted sexually, via infected body fluids and even from mother to unborn child

In the UK, recent statistics show for the first time, that the number of diagnosed cases in heterosexual relationships exceeds those of gay relationships. That is not by any means cause to assume that unprotected penetrative gay sex is safer than heterosexual penetrative sex. Statistically it would also seem that the age range of people being diagnosed is becoming younger. But, lets not be fooled. This is not an 'odds' game. While new drugs have helped the treatment of immune deficiency, not too many people realise how severe and debilitating in other ways that the regimen can be. Neither are the drugs a panacea for all diagnosed cases

What of the other sexually transmitted infections? The incidence of gonorrhoea have soared, and all you might read about it is a seventh-column half-inch item buried somewhere in a newspaper.

The purpose of writing this article is not to scare anybody into celibacy; rather it is to disperse some very Dangerous Delusions that are specifically related to gender issues

Since neither sex nor gender are at the extreme ends of a spectrum, there are gradations between both male and female and masculine and feminine. In addition, sexual preferences can be heterosexual, homosexual, bisexual or asexual.

We know that many people who are either transsexual or transvestite do not seek sexual activity in that role and there is no safer form of protection than abstinence. Equally, many people cross dress to express an emotional rather than a sexual aspect of their personality and find great pleasure in the ability to be dressed in the gender of their choice, be it on their own, with friends or with family.

For many years I have heard numerous people state that gender has little to do with sexual preferences, and while in essence that may be true for the majority there is still a substantial proportion of cross gender individuals who, be they heterosexual, bisexual or homosexual have a different view of their sexuality when cross dressed.

The surveys that I have seen have been rather too biased to be of any real consequence. I suspect that the proportion of gay cross dressers is probably less than the population in general, but the proportion of bisexual cross dressers may be greater. It should also be remembered that heterosexuality is probably the greatest proportion of all.

Irrespective of whether a person refers to themselves as male, female, TG, CD, TS (Post or pre op) TV, Fetishist or any other term the risk is the same. The terminology an individual chooses for himself or herself is not the issue at stake. Sexually transmitted infections do not discriminate between male and female neither is there a discrimination based upon sexual preferences. The risk upon that basis is equal. Sexual activity is of course not the only method of contacting infections or diseases of this nature, however for the purposes of this article and in order not to detract from the central issue I propose limiting my comments to sexually transmitted infections

I am all too aware of situations where a person who cross dresses, in whatever form that takes will for example smoke or drink when they are in their chosen role but not otherwise (when they revert to the role in which most people see them). In the same way I am aware of many instances where a cross dresser will declare themselves to be heterosexual when in reality they may be bisexual. The reasoning being that for whatever period of time their 'adopted' or psychological role is opposite to that of their sexual partner, they will determine and think of themselves as heterosexual – the adopted role giving licence to the denial of their physical gender.

Also quite common is the complete psychological 'switching' of roles, so that when the individual is dressed as a female, they will totally deny their maleness, male attitudes and male gender. In their mind and dress, they are a totally different person. The man who is say called 'Bill' totally adopts the role of a female, say 'Jill' for the length of time he is cross dressed. It is not unusual that the person will only wish to be seen or acknowledged by their associates in one particular role. People who know 'Jill' will never meet 'Bill' and vice versa.

Let us assume that 'Bill' neither smokes nor drinks. One would assume that 'Jill' likewise would refrain. That is not always the case. The same will sometimes apply equally to sexual activity. 'Bill' might never think of going with another man or woman outside of his living relationship but 'Bill', dressed as, and in the role of 'Jill' might. Would it not be the ultimate acceptance of 'Jill' as a wholly recognised and accepted 'female'?

It is at this point that the Dangerous Delusions come into being. As strange as it might seem in the harsh glare of print, the division between the two aspects of the same person is sometimes so pronounced that on the spur of the moment 'Jill' forgets the reality of 'Bill'. Forgets or chooses not to assess the implications that unprotected sex may have on 'Bill' and his life. In fact forgets the implications of unprotected sex altogether. For that period of time 'Bill', in Jill's mind simply does not exist.

As with any other group, some transvestites and transsexual people are so homophobic that it does not occur to them that they, in their female role could be attractive to women, however, there are many who fantasise about being lesbian or having a 'lesbian' relationship.

We all know that humans take risks, frequently with dire results. Sometimes these judgments are made in a calculated manner. That is seldom the case with an unexpected sexual encounter. Decisions are made at a time when the rush of blood is not always to the brain. It is easy to think, "I'm Jill, not Bill", but to steal part of a saying of Mr Churchill "But in the morning you will still be 'Bill'."

Sexually transmitted infections have not gone away, they have just not held the headlines. The term AIDS to most people does not have the same impact now as it had ten years ago. People have AIDS related disorders, nobody dies of AIDS. Whichever way the words are laid out before you the risks and the possible effects are the same.

Nobody can afford to be complacent and HIV is not the only sexually transmitted infection by a very long chalk. It is though, for obvious reasons, the one most feared by the majority of people. There are means of protection, such as condoms which, in the heat of the moment are, unfortunately, all too often forgotten. Not using a condom 'just that once' can literally be a matter of life or death. Not just to that individual but to those closest to him, those he is most intimate with. Not quite so obvious is the risk of using condoms and lubricants together. Oil based lubricants can damage the rubber causing the condom to fail. Water based lubricants such as KY Jelly, TLC, Boots water based lubricants will not adversely affect the structure of the condom. One's hands should also be free of oil-based substances, such as sun tan or body oils.

So, whether you are in the role of male, female, 'Jill'/'Bill' naked or clothed; irrespective of whether you think of yourself as straight, gay, lesbian, bisexual or heterosexual; whether you are with a male or a female YOU ARE NOT IMMUNE.

I recently heard a chilling tale of a woman with AIDS. Asked if she used condoms her reply was "NO, I can't be infected twice so why should I bother".

Please don't be deluded into thinking that 'Jill' is physically protected from anything that 'Bill' might contract, or of course *vice versa*. Sounds far fetched? In the heat of the situation it is not so unusual. It falls in line with the view of 'It always happens to somebody else' There is a statistical view that if you know somebody who has won a big prize on the National Lottery, it is highly unlikely that you will have the same fortune. That being the case, if you know somebody who is HIV positive, do you think that places you at a lesser risk? I think not.

At the time of going to print, it is estimated that 2 million people have died from HIV-related diseases, and the rate of infection is 15,000 (yes, fifteen thousand) per day.★

What am I trying to put across to you is a desire for you to be aware, for you to protect yourself. ALL OF YOURSELF, ALL OF THE TIME, and in whatever your birth, rightful, adopted or chosen gender may be. Hopefully that way you will also be protective of your sexual partner(s).

★UNAIDS statistics.

Further information may be obtained from:
Terrence Higgins Trust,
52-54, Grays Inn Road, London WC1X 8JE
020 7831 0330
(Also in Bath, Birmingham, Brighton, Bristol, Coventry, Leeds & Oxford) http://www.tht.org.uk

National AIDS Helpline, 0800 567123
Deals with all sexually transmitted diseases

HELP ON THE NET
Society of Health Advisers in Sexually Transmitted Diseases (SHASTD) http://www.shastd.org.uk/index.htm

National AIDS Manual http://www.aidsmap.com

Durex, Condom Manufacturer, http://www.durex.com

Condomania, Suppliers of Condoms,
http://www.condoms4u.com

Positive Nation, HIV Magazine,
http://www.positivenation.co.uk

Medisearch (Search engine specific to the UK medical sector)
http://www.medisearch.co.uk

Public Health Laboratory Service
Current news and statistics on STI's including HIV in the UK. http://www.phls.co.uk

Further Reading

Periodicals
Members only
Beaumont Magazine
Beaumont Society, 27, Old Gloucester Street, London WC1N 3XX
Crosstalk
Northern Concord, PO Box 258, Manchester M60 1LN
On general sale:
Tranny Guide
WayOut Publishing, P.O.Box 70, Enfield, EN1 2AE
Tapestry
International Foundation for Gender Education, PO Box 540229, Waltham, Massachusetts, 02454-0229, USA
TransLife
TransCare, PO Box 3, Basildon, Essex SS14 1PT
Repartee
Rose's (Dept BT) P.O.Box 186, Barnsley S73 0YT

General Reading
Cross Dressing, Sex and Gender, Vern & Bonnie Bullough
(1993) University of Pennsylvania Press.
Transgender Warriors, Leslie Feinberg
(1997) Boston: Beacon Press
The Gender Paradox. Jed Bland,
(1993) Derby TV/TS Group, Belper, Derby.
Insights into transvestism, transsexualism and other gender presentations
(2002) TransCare, PO Box 3, Basildon, Essex SS14 1PT
Normal - Transsexual CEO's, Crossdressing Cops and Hermaphrodites With Attitude,
Amy Bloom, (2003) London: Bloomsbury

Men in Petticoats. Peter Farrer,
(1990) Kam Publications Garstang
In Female Disguise. Peter Farrer,
(1990) Kam Publications Garstang
Sex, Gender & Sexuality Dr. Tracie O'Keefe
(1999) Turnaround Press
Finding the Real Me: True Tales of Sex & Gender Diversity
Edited by Dr. Tracie O'Keefe and Katrina Fox
(2003) Jossey Bass, division of Wiley
My Husband Betty, Helen Boyd,
(2004) Thunder's Mouth Press
Male femaling: A grounded theory approach to Cross-dressing and Sex-changing, Richard Ekins (1997) Routledge
Vested Interests: Cross-dressing and Cultural Anxiety, Garber, M, (1992) London: Penguin
The Third Sex: Kathoey, Thailand's Ladyboys, Richard Totman (2003) Souvenir Press

Changing Ones: Third and Fourth Genders in Native North America, Will Roscoe (2000) St. Martin's Press

Evolution's Rainbow: Diversity, Gender and Sexuality in Nature and People, Joan Roughgarden
(2004) University of California Press

Produced for the Beaumont Trust
by the Derby TV/TS Group,
Belper, Derby, England.
Printed by Intype Libra Ltd
Units 3-4, Elm Grove Industrial Estate,
Wimbledon, London SW19 4HE
2004